LIGHT RECIPES

by
Jean Paré

Dedication

Take a step in the light direction.

Cover Photo

LIGHT RECIPES

Fourth Printing March 1994

I.S.B.N. 1-895455-12-X

Published and Distributed by
Company's Coming Publishing Limited
Box 8037, Station "F"
Edmonton, Alberta, Canada
T6H 4N9

**Published Simultaneously in
Canada and the United States of America**

Printed in Canada

Company's Coming Cookbooks
by Jean Paré

COMPANY'S COMING SERIES
English

HARD COVER
- JEAN PARÉ'S FAVORITES
  - Volume One

SOFT COVER
- 150 DELICIOUS SQUARES
- CASSEROLES
- MUFFINS & MORE
- SALADS
- APPETIZERS
- DESSERTS
- SOUPS & SANDWICHES
- HOLIDAY ENTERTAINING
- COOKIES
- VEGETABLES
- MAIN COURSES
- PASTA
- CAKES
- BARBECUES
- DINNERS OF THE WORLD
- LUNCHES
- PIES
- LIGHT RECIPES
- MICROWAVE COOKING
- PRESERVES
- LIGHT CASSEROLES (Sept. '94)

PINT SIZE BOOKS
English

SOFT COVER
- FINGER FOOD
- PARTY PLANNING
- BUFFETS

JEAN PARÉ LIVRES DE CUISINE
French

SOFT COVER
- 150 DÉLICIEUX CARRÉS
- LES CASSEROLES
- MUFFINS ET PLUS
- LES DÎNERS
- LES BARBECUES
- LES TARTES
- DÉLICES DES FÊTES
- RECETTES LÉGÈRES
- LES SALADES
- LA CUISSON AU MICRO-ONDES
- LES PÂTES
- LES CONSERVES
- LES CASSEROLES LÉGÈRES (sept '94)

table of Contents

the Jean Paré story

Jean Paré was born and raised during the Great Depression in Irma, a small rural town in eastern Alberta, Canada. She grew up understanding that the combination of family, friends and home cooking is the essence of a good life. Jean learned from her mother, Ruby Elford, to appreciate good cooking and was encouraged by her father, Edward Elford, who praised even her earliest attempts. When she left home she took with her many acquired family recipes, her love of cooking and her intriguing desire to read recipe books like novels!

While raising a family of four, Jean was always busy in her kitchen preparing delicious, tasty treats and savory meals for family and friends of all ages. Her reputation flourished as the mom who would happily feed the neighborhood.

In 1963, when her children had all reached school age, Jean volunteered to cater to the 50th anniversary of the Vermilion School of Agriculture, now Lakeland College. Working out of her home, Jean prepared a dinner for over 1000 people which launched a flourishing catering operation that continued for over eighteen years. During that time she was provided with countless opportunities to test new ideas with immediate feedback – resulting in empty plates and contented customers! Whether preparing cocktail sandwiches for a house party or serving a hot meal for 1500 people, Jean Paré earned a reputation for good food, courteous service and reasonable prices.

"Why don't you write a cookbook?" Time and again, as requests for her recipes mounted, Jean was asked that question. Jean's response was to team up with her son Grant Lovig in the fall of 1980 to form Company's Coming Publishing Limited. April 14, 1981, marked the debut of "150 DELICIOUS SQUARES", the first Company's Coming cookbook in what soon would become Canada's most popular cookbook series. Jean released a new title each year for the first six years. The pace quickened and by 1987 the company had begun publishing two titles each year.

Jean Paré's operation has grown from the early days of working out of a spare bedroom in her home to operating a large and fully equipped test kitchen in Vermilion, Alberta, near the home she and her husband Larry built. Full time staff has grown steadily to include marketing personnel located in major cities across Canada plus selected U.S. markets. Home Office is located in Edmonton, Alberta where distribution, accounting and administration functions are headquartered in the company's own recently constructed 20,000 square foot facility. Company's Coming cookbooks are now distributed throughout Canada and the United States plus numerous overseas markets. Translation of the series to the Spanish and French languages began in 1990. Pint Size Books followed in 1993, offering a smaller, less expensive format focusing on more specialized topics. The recipes continued in the familiar and trusted Company's Coming style.

Jean Paré's approach to cooking has always called for easy-to-follow recipes using mostly common, affordable ingredients. Her wonderful collection of time-honored recipes, many of which are family heirlooms, is a welcome addition to any kitchen. That's why we say: "taste the tradition".

Foreword

Light is the word. The recipes in this cookbook have been created and tested with a step in the "light" direction. This is not a diet book or a medical reference book but a book which features light and healthy recipes. The many trade-offs used help you cut down your intake of calories, cholesterol, sodium and fat while allowing you to enjoy nutritious, delicious results. If you are watching your cholesterol, you may wish to choose from several recipes which omit eggs and saturated fats and yet are surprisingly full of flavor. Many recipes omit salt to assist those who would like to reduce the intake of sodium in their diet.

For your next dinner party, start the meal off with a steaming bowl of Vegetable Soup followed by Sesame Chicken served with Carrot Magic and Zucchini. Surprise your guests and family with a scrumptious dessert such as Chocolate Truffles or Red Bottom Pudding Pie. Rummy Melon is another refreshing choice.

A Nutrition Guide follows every recipe which gives calories, cholesterol, sodium and fat contents for each portion or serving. Whether you are on a restricted diet or simply prefer healthy and sensible eating, the recipes in this book help you to make your meal planning choices easy, while still using mostly common, affordable ingredients.

Jean Paré

The key to healthy eating is balance and moderation. However, keeping track of calories, cholesterol, sodium and fat in our diet can be quite a challenge for most people. This book on light recipes can surely make your job easier. Each recipe has been carefully analyzed with expertise using the most up-dated version (1991) of the Canadian Nutrient File from Health and Welfare Canada, which is based upon the United States Department of Agriculture (USDA) Nutrient Data Base. With such guidance, you can plan a healthy diet through selecting a variety of foods from this book.

Margaret Ng, B.Sc. (Hon), M.A.
Registered Dietitian

Glossary

Calorie: A unit measure of energy which is required for healthy living.

Cholesterol: Only found in animal, fish and shellfish sources of food, not in plant foods. Guidelines for cholesterol intake generally suggest 300 mg or less per day. Total cholesterol count is given in each recipe to make you aware of your intake.

Fat: Recommended fat intake is generally 30% or less of total daily intake of calories. For example, if your total caloric intake per day is between 1800 and 2200, then total grams of fat per day should be 60 to 70 g. To determine you intake of fat calories, remember 1 gram of fat is approximately 9 calories. Do not be confused with % MF (milk fat) or % BF (butter fat) as seen on the labels of dairy products. This percentage refers to weight of fat in the product. For example, a cheese with 31% MF (or BF) may have 75% of its calories result from the fat content.

Pepper: A pepper grinder is a great utensil. Fresh pepper will perk up any food which is on the bland side.

Salt and Sodium: It is recommended to limit the intake of sodium to 2000 to 3000 mg per day. Salt consists of 40 percent sodium. Sodium is also high in processed foods. Sodium found in 1 tsp. (5 mL) salt is approximately 2000 mg. Prepare your dishes without adding salt or MSG (monosodium glutamate). If on a sodium-restricted diet, use a salt substitute.

Salt Substitutes: Use sodium-free herbs and spices to enhance flavors of foods. For fish, try a sprinkle of basil, dill, curry or tarragon. For fruit, try allspice, cinnamon, ginger or nutmeg. For meat or poultry, cook with bay leaf, chili powder, curry, garlic, oregano, basil, thyme or wine. For salads and vegetables, try freshly ground pepper, basil, celery seed, chives, dill, garlic, oregano, tarragon, thyme or fresh lemon juice.

Servings: As a guide to determine servings of meat, a rule of thumb is to use 4 oz. (113 g) of boneless fresh meat per person, which equals 3 oz. (84 g) of cooked meat. This is approximately the size of a deck of playing cards. A scale is a big asset.

Soup: Most people find it difficult to make tasty soup without salt. If you make your own stock, you will get more flavor by boiling it down. Experiment with spices for subtle tastes. If you prepare your soups without salt, you may want to try a sprinkle of salt or salt substitute just before eating.

Sweetener: A liquid sugar substitute has been used for testing some of the recipes in this book. Sugar may be used if you prefer. However, to create the same degree of sweetness you will need to use about 4 times more sugar than the substitute. Total calories will also increase. One teaspoon (5 mL) of sugar has 15 Calories.

Delightful little morsels.

Large mushrooms	18	18
Finely minced onion	3 tbsp.	50 mL
Finely chopped celery	3 tbsp.	50 mL
Reserved mushroom stems, finely chopped		
Garlic powder	1/4 tsp.	1 mL
Water	1/3 cup	75 mL
Dry bread crumbs	1/2 cup	125 mL
Grated Parmesan cheese	2 tbsp.	30 mL
Parsley flakes	1 tsp.	5 mL
Salt	1/4 tsp.	1 mL
Pepper	1/8 tsp.	0.5 mL
Poultry seasoning	1/8 tsp.	0.5 mL
Bacon bits, crushed to a powder	1 tsp.	5 mL

Remove mushroom stems carefully and reserve.

Place next 5 ingredients in frying pan. Bring to a boil. Cover and simmer gently about 5 to 6 minutes until celery is cooked. Add a touch more water as needed. When celery is cooked, drain.

Add bread crumbs, cheese, parsley, salt, pepper and poultry seasoning. Stir well. Stuff mushroom caps. Arrange on baking sheet.

Sprinkle with crushed bacon bits. Bake in 350°F (175°C) oven for 15 to 20 minutes. Serve hot. Makes 18.

Pictured on page 17.

NUTRITION GUIDE	**1 stuffed mushroom contains:**	
	Energy	21 Calories (86 kJ)
	Cholesterol	trace
	Sodium	104 mg
	Fat	trace

BROILED GRAPEFRUIT

An ideal breakfast treat. These may be wrapped in foil and barbecued until hot.

Grapefruit, halved	2	2
Brown sugar (see Note)	4 tbsp.	60 mL
Water	2 tbsp.	30 mL
Imitation brandy extract	2 tsp.	10 mL
Maraschino cherries	4	4

Remove seeds from grapefruit. Loosen fruit sections from membrane. Arrange on broiler tray.

In small cup mix brown sugar, water and brandy flavoring. If too dry, a wee bit of water can be added. Divide among grapefruit halves. Smooth over surface with back of spoon. Broil about 3 minutes.

Place cherry in center. Pour any juice left in pan over top. Makes 4 servings.

N U T R I T I O N G U I D E	1 serving contains:	
	Energy	84 Calories (350 kJ)
	Cholesterol	0 mg
	Sodium	3 mg
	Fat	trace

Note: To reduce calories further, replace brown sugar with same amount of brown sugar substitute. Water should not be needed.

TUNA TOAST POINTS

This is an appetizer where you will find one is never enough. Tuna may be replaced with crab. It will have a higher sodium and cholesterol count.

Light salad dressing (or mayonnaise)	1 cup	225 mL
Curry powder	1/2 tsp.	2 mL
Canned white tuna, water packed, drained	6 1/2 oz.	184 g
White bread slices, crust removed	12	12
Grated low-fat medium Cheddar cheese (less than 21% MF)	1/2 cup	125 mL

(continued on next page)

Mix salad dressing and curry powder. Add tuna. Stir.

Cut bread slices in half diagonally. Arrange on cookie sheet. Toast 1 side under broiler about 1 minute. Remove from oven. Turn bread over. Spread untoasted sides with tuna mixture.

Sprinkle cheese in center of each piece. Broil about 2 to 2¹/₂ minutes, until lightly browned. Makes 24.

NUTRITION GUIDE	1 toast point contains:	
	Energy	77 Calories (324 kJ)
	Cholesterol	4 mg
	Sodium	204 mg
	Fat	4 g

MOCK GUACAMOLE

Mock, to be sure and a good imitation. Serve with tostados, tortilla chips, corn chips or fresh raw vegetables.

Frozen peas, cooked	**2 cups**	**450 mL**
Chopped onion	**2 tbsp.**	**30 mL**
Lemon juice	**2 tbsp.**	**30 mL**
Salt	**¹/₂ tsp.**	**2 mL**
Pepper	**¹/₄ tsp.**	**1 mL**
Garlic powder	**¹/₄ tsp.**	**1 mL**
Cayenne pepper	**¹/₄ tsp.**	**1 mL**
Medium tomato, diced	**1**	**1**

Smooth first 7 ingredients in food processor.

Place diced tomato on paper towel to drain. Stir into first ingredients. Makes about 1¹/₂ cups (350 mL).

Pictured on page 17.

NUTRITION GUIDE	1 tbsp./15 mL contains:	
	Energy	13 Calories (54 kJ)
	Cholesterol	trace
	Sodium	69 mg
	Fat	trace

MOCK CHILI GUACAMOLE: Just add ¹/₄ tsp. (1 mL) chili powder for a very delicious touch.

SPINACH DIP

Lower in calories and fat than regular similar dips. Good flavor.

Low-fat cottage cheese (less than 1% MF)	1 cup	225 mL
Light salad dressing (or mayonnaise)	1 cup	225 mL
Lemon juice	2 tbsp.	30 mL
Chopped onion	1/3 cup	75 mL
Frozen chopped spinach, thawed, drained, blotted dry	10 oz.	284 g
Parsley flakes	2 tsp.	10 mL

Place first 4 ingredients in blender. Blend smooth. Turn into bowl.

Stir in spinach and parsley. This is good served warm and also when it cools. Makes 2²/₃ cups (600 mL).

Pictured on page 17.

NUTRITION GUIDE	1 tbsp./15 mL contains:	
	Energy	23 Calories (98 kJ)
	Cholesterol	trace
	Sodium	78 mg
	Fat	2 g

Variation: May be used to fill a hollowed out round bread loaf, then wrap in foil and heat in 300°F (150°C) oven for 2 hours. Cut up removed bread to use as dippers.

ORIENTAL MEATBALLS

A fantastic nibbly with a great dipping sauce. Doubles as a main dish.

MEATBALLS

Lean ground beef	1 lb.	454 g
Water	1/2 cup	125 mL
Dry bread crumbs	1/2 cup	125 mL
Pepper	1/4 tsp.	1 mL
Onion powder	1/4 tsp.	1 mL
Garlic powder	1/4 tsp.	1 mL
Canned water chestnuts, drained, very finely chopped	5 oz.	142 mL

PEACH DIP

Babyfood strained peaches, no added sugar	2 x 4¹/₂ oz.	2 x 128 mL
Cider vinegar	2 tbsp.	30 mL
Liquid sweetener	2 tsp.	10 mL

(continued on next page)

Meatballs: Combine all 7 ingredients in bowl. Mix well. Divide into 4 equal balls. Now divide each ball into 10 meatballs. Arrange on baking sheet which has been coated with no-stick cooking spray. Cook in 375°F (190°C) oven for about 15 to 20 minutes. Yield: 40 meatballs.

Peach Dip: Put all 3 ingredients into bowl. Stir. Use hot or cold as a dip for meatballs. Makes 1 cup (225 mL).

NUTRITION GUIDE	1 meatball plus 1 tsp./5mL dip contains:	
	Energy	35 Calories (144 kJ)
	Cholesterol	6 mg
	Sodium	19 mg
	Fat	2 g

LITTLE HAM BITES

These wee balls also contain turkey. Use as an appetizer or main course.

Canned ham flakes (33% reduced salt)	**6¹/₂ oz.**	**184 g**
Ground raw turkey	**¹/₂ lb.**	**225 g**
Chopped green onion	**¹/₄ cup**	**50 mL**
Canned water chestnuts, drained,	**¹/₂ cup**	**125 mL**
finely chopped		
Dry bread crumbs	**¹/₄ cup**	**50 mL**
Large egg, fork beaten	**1**	**1**
Water	**1 tbsp.**	**15 mL**
Garlic powder	**¹/₄ tsp.**	**1 mL**

Combine all 8 ingredients in bowl. Mix well. A bit more water may be added if too dry, but it shouldn't be too soft. Shape into marble size balls about 1 inch (2.5 cm) in diameter. Arrange on pan that has been sprayed with no-stick cooking spray. Bake in 425°F (220°C) oven for 15 minutes. Serve hot with picks and Mustard Sauce, page 69, if desired. These may be chilled and reheated. Makes about 60.

NUTRITION GUIDE	1 ham bite contains:	
	Energy	14 Calories (57 kJ)
	Cholesterol	8 mg
	Sodium	29 mg
	Fat	1 g

FRUIT PUNCH

A good thirst quencher.

Prepared orange juice, unsweetened	¹/₂ cup	125 mL
Pineapple juice, unsweetened	¹/₄ cup	60 mL
Lemon juice	1 tbsp.	15 mL
Diet Seven Up soft drink	1 cup	225 mL

Have all ingredients chilled. Combine orange, pineapple and lemon juices in pitcher. Add Seven Up. Stir lightly. Diet ginger ale may be used instead of Seven Up, but the color of the punch is dull rather than bright. Makes 2 servings.

NUTRITION GUIDE	**1 serving contains:**	
	Energy	49 Calories (207 kJ)
	Cholesterol	0 mg
	Sodium	9 mg
	Fat	trace

LEMONADE

An old timer without sugar. A good thirst quencher.

Large lemons	2	2
Medium orange	1	1
Water	4 cups	900 mL
Liquid sweetener	2 tbsp.	30 mL
Grenadine syrup (optional)	1¹/₂ tsp.	7 mL

Squeeze lemons and orange. Remove any seeds. Pour into pitcher. Add water, sweetener and grenadine. Stir. Makes 4²/₃ cups (1.05 L).

Pictured on page 35.

NUTRITION GUIDE	**1 cup/225 mL contains:**	
	Energy	31 Calories (128 kJ)
	Cholesterol	0 mg
	Sodium	2 mg
	Fat	trace

A popular appetizer without so much cholesterol and calories. Serve with crackers.

Low fat cottage cheese (less than 1% MF), rinsed and drained well	2 cups	450 mL
Margarine, softened	¹/₂ cup	125 mL
Grated low-fat sharp Cheddar cheese (less than 21% MF)	2 cups	450 mL
Chopped pimiento	1 tbsp.	15 mL
Chopped green pepper	1 tbsp.	15 mL
Onion flakes	1¹/₂ tbsp.	25 mL
Worcestershire sauce	1 tbsp.	15 mL
Lemon juice	2 tsp.	10 mL
Cayenne pepper	¹/₈ tsp.	0.5 mL
Chopped fresh parsley	¹/₂ cup	125 mL

Place cottage cheese and margarine in blender or food processor. Process until smooth.

Combine next 7 ingredients in large bowl. Add blender contents. Mix well. Chill several hours or overnight.

Shape into ball. Roll in parsley. Chill. Makes 3¹/₂ cups (800 mL).

Pictured on page 17.

NUTRITION GUIDE	**1 tbsp./15 mL contains:**	
	Energy	34 Calories (142 kJ)
	Cholesterol	3 mg
	Sodium	127 mg
	Fat	3 g

A quick way to be an actor is to break a leg. You'll be in a cast for months.

TUNA SPREAD

Serve with a small knife so all guests can help themselves. Tasty.

Canned white flaked tuna, water packed, drained	6$^{1}/_{2}$ oz.	184 g
Finely chopped onion	$^{1}/_{4}$ cup	60 mL
Ground walnuts, very finely chopped	3 tbsp.	50 mL
Lemon juice	1 tsp.	5 mL
Salt	$^{1}/_{4}$ tsp.	1 mL
Pepper	$^{1}/_{4}$ tsp.	1 mL
Light salad dressing (or mayonnaise)	6 tbsp.	90 mL

Combine all 7 ingredients in bowl. Mix well. Chill until needed. Serve with assorted crackers. Makes 1$^{1}/_{3}$ cups (300 mL).

NUTRITION GUIDE	1tbsp./15 mL contains:	
	Energy	30 Calories (126 kJ)
	Cholesterol	3 mg
	Sodium	93 mg
	Fat	2 g

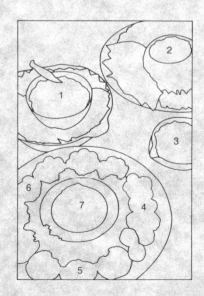

Good flavor with an economical smoked accent. Serve with crackers. May be rolled in chopped walnuts and pecans if you aren't watching calories and fat.

Low-fat cottage cheese (less than 1% MF)	1 cup	225 mL
Margarine, softened	1/4 cup	50 mL
Grated onion	1 tbsp.	15 mL
Lemon juice	1 tbsp.	15 mL
Horseradish	1 tsp.	5 mL
Salt	1/4 tsp.	1 mL
Liquid smoke	1 tsp.	5 mL
Canned salmon (red is best), drained	2 x 7 1/2 oz.	2 x 213 g
Chopped fresh parsley	1/4 cup	60 mL

Combine first 7 ingredients in small mixing bowl. Beat until smooth.

Remove round bones and dark skin from salmon. Add salmon and beat in slowly. Pack into shallow serving dish.

Sprinkle with parsley. Chill until ready to serve. Makes 2 2/3 cups (600 mL).

Pictured on page 17.

NUTRITION GUIDE	1 tbsp./15 mL contains:	
	Energy	30 Calories (127 kJ)
	Cholesterol	3 mg
	Sodium	94 mg
	Fat	2 g

Tall people don't rise as early as short people because they're longer in bed.

SHRIMP DIP

This will gratify your longing for a tasty munchie. Serve with crackers.

Low-fat cottage cheese (less than 1% MF)	1 cup	225 mL
Margarine, softened	1/4 cup	60 mL
Light salad dressing (or mayonnaise)	1/4 cup	60 mL
Chili sauce	2 tsp.	10 mL
Lemon juice	1 tsp.	5 mL
Worcestershire sauce	1 tsp.	5 mL
Dill weed	1/4 tsp.	1 mL
Garlic powder	1/16 tsp.	0.5 mL
Canned broken shrimp, rinsed and drained	4 oz.	113 g

Combine all 9 ingredients in blender. Blend smooth. Chill until needed. This won't firm up when chilled because no cream cheese has been added. It is firm enough for dipping. Makes 2 cups (450 mL).

NUTRITION GUIDE	1 tbsp./15 mL contains:	
	Energy	28 Calories (118 kJ)
	Cholesterol	6 mg
	Sodium	75 mg
	Fat	2 g

STUFFED CUCUMBER

Pretty slices on a cracker.

Low-fat cottage cheese (less than 1% MF), drained	3/4 cup	175 mL
Margarine, softened	3 tbsp.	50 mL
Chives, chopped	2 tsp.	10 mL
Beef bouillon packet (35% less salt)	1 x 1/4 oz.	1 x 6.5 g
Worcestershire sauce, generous measure	1/4 tsp.	1 mL
Cayenne pepper (optional)	1/16 tsp.	0.5 mL
Medium cucumbers (about 9 inches in length), scored with fork, centers hollowed out	2	2
Round crackers	40	40

(continued on next page)

Combine first 6 ingredients on small plate. Mash with fork until thoroughly blended together.

Stuff cucumbers. Chill for 2 hours. Cut into scant ½ inch (1 cm) slices. Place each slice on cracker. Makes about 40.

Pictured on page 17.

<table>
<tr><td rowspan="5">N U T R I T I O N
G U I D E</td><td colspan="2">1 slice on cracker contains:</td></tr>
<tr><td>Energy</td><td>30 Calories (123 kJ)</td></tr>
<tr><td>Cholesterol</td><td>trace</td></tr>
<tr><td>Sodium</td><td>78 mg</td></tr>
<tr><td>Fat</td><td>2 g</td></tr>
</table>

MEATBALLS

Whether using for the fantastic appetizer it is, or for a main course, this is guaranteed to please.

Lean ground beef	**2 lbs.**	**900 g**
Onion powder	**½ tsp.**	**2 mL**
Water	**½ cup**	**125 mL**
Dry bread crumbs	**½ cup**	**125 mL**
Pepper	**½ tsp.**	**2 mL**
RED SAUCE		
Tomato paste	**1 × 5½ oz.**	**1 × 156 mL**
Water	**¾ cup**	**175 mL**
Vinegar	**4½ tsp.**	**22 mL**
Liquid sweetener	**1½ tsp.**	**7 mL**
Worcestershire sauce	**¾ tsp.**	**4 mL**
Onion powder	**¼ tsp.**	**1 mL**

Mix first 5 ingredients in bowl. Shape into 1 inch (2.5 cm) balls. Arrange on baking sheet. Cook in 450°F (230°C) oven about 15 minutes, until browned. Makes 80 meatballs.

Red Sauce: Place all 6 ingredients in small saucepan. Heat and stir until it boils. Pour over meatballs or serve separately as a dip. Makes 1½ cups (350 mL).

<table>
<tr><td rowspan="5">N U T R I T I O N
G U I D E</td><td colspan="2">1 sauced meatball contains:</td></tr>
<tr><td>Energy</td><td>29 Calories (122 kJ)</td></tr>
<tr><td>Cholesterol</td><td>6 mg</td></tr>
<tr><td>Sodium</td><td>15 mg</td></tr>
<tr><td>Fat</td><td>2 g</td></tr>
</table>

TUNA QUICHE

A perfect starter for a meal. Also good for lunch.

Egg white (large)	1	1
All-purpose flour	2½ tbsp.	40 mL
Evaporated skim milk	1¼ cups	275 mL
Cayenne pepper	⅛ tsp.	0.5 mL
Paprika	⅛ tsp.	0.5 mL
Canned white tuna, water packed, drained	6½ oz.	184 g
Unbaked 9 inch (22 cm) pie shell, see page 46	1	1
Grated low-fat farmers cheese (less than 21% MF)	1 cup	225 mL
Chopped green onion	2 tbsp.	30 mL

Beat egg white in small bowl until frothy. Add flour. Beat until smooth. Mix in milk, cayenne pepper and paprika.

Spread tuna in bottom of pie shell. Sprinkle with cheese and green onion. Pour milk mixture over top. Bake in 350°F (175°C) oven for about 50 to 60 minutes until set. Remove from oven. Makes 8 appetizer servings.

Pictured on page 17.

NUTRITION GUIDE	⅛ **quiche contains:**	
	Energy	239 Calories (999 kJ)
	Cholesterol	22 mg
	Sodium	274 mg
	Fat	11 g

Variation: This also may be used to make 16 to 18 quiche tarts or 36 tiny quiche. For tarts it is easier to mix all ingredients together before filling tart shells.

DILL DIP

Enjoy this easy to make dip with assorted vegetables.

Light salad dressing (or mayonnaise)	1 cup	225 mL
Low-fat plain yogurt (less than 1% MF)	1 cup	225 mL
Onion powder	¼ tsp.	1 mL
Chopped chives	2 tsp.	10 mL
Dill weed	2 tsp.	10 mL
Celery salt	¼ tsp.	1 mL

(continued on next page)

Mix all 6 ingredients in small bowl. Chill for at least 1 hour before using. Makes 2 cups (450 mL).

NUTRITION GUIDE	1 tbsp. /15 mL contains:	
	Energy	27 Calories (112 kJ)
	Cholesterol	trace
	Sodium	83 mg
	Fat	2 g

CRAB DIP

Instead of the usual cream cheese, this recipe uses low-fat cottage cheese. Make it ahead, ready to heat when needed. Water packed tuna can be used instead of crabmeat for lower sodium and cholesterol.

Canned crabmeat, drained, cartilage removed	5 oz.	142 g
Low-fat cottage cheese (less than 1% MF)	1 cup	225 mL
Horseradish	1/2 tsp.	2 mL
Salt	1/4 tsp.	1 mL
Skim milk	1 tbsp.	15 mL
Margarine, softened	1/4 cup	50 mL
Onion powder	1/4 tsp.	1 mL
Sliced almonds	1/4 cup	50 mL

Combine first 7 ingredients in blender. Blend smooth. May be beaten in bowl instead of blending. Add more horseradish to taste. Turn into 1 quart (1 L) casserole. Smooth top.

Place almonds in 375°F (190°C) oven for about 4 to 6 minutes to brown. Remove and sprinkle over casserole. Return to oven and cook for about 20 minutes until hot. Makes 2 1/8 cups (480 mL).

NUTRITION GUIDE	1 tbsp. /15 mL contains:	
	Energy	25 Calories (104 kJ)
	Cholesterol	trace
	Sodium	92 mg
	Fat	2 g

CHICKEN SANDWICH

A good full sandwich. For fewer calories, half the amount of chicken may be used.

Whole wheat bread slices (100%)	2	2
Margarine	1½ tsp.	7 mL
Cooked chicken breast (skinned and boned)	2 oz.	56 g
Pepper, sprinkle		
Lettuce leaves	2	2
Light salad dressing (or mayonnaise)	1½ tsp.	7 mL

Spread bread slices with margarine. On 1 slice layer chicken, pepper and lettuce.

Spread second bread slice with salad dressing and place on lettuce. Cut in half diagonally. Serves 1.

Pictured on page 35.

NUTRITION GUIDE	1 sandwich contains:	
	Energy	308 Calories (1288 kJ)
	Cholesterol	50 mg
	Sodium	470 mg
	Fat	8 g

BANANA LOAF

Dark and full of flecks. Delicious flavor.

Mashed bananas (3 medium)	1 cup	225 mL
Baking soda	1 tsp.	5 mL
Large eggs	2	2
Margarine, softened	¼ cup	60 mL
Brown sugar, packed	(1/4)c cup	225 mL
All-purpose flour	1½ cups	350 mL
Baking powder	1½ tsp.	7 mL
Salt	¼ tsp.	1 mL

(continued on next page)

In small bowl stir mashed banana and baking soda together. Set aside.

Beat eggs in small mixing bowl until frothy.

Cream margarine and sugar in large mixing bowl. Add ½ eggs. Beat to mix. Add second ½ eggs. Beat in. Stir in mashed banana.

Add flour, baking powder and salt. Stir to moisten. Spoon into 9 x 5 inch (23 x 12 cm) loaf pan that has been sprayed with no-stick cooking spray. Bake in 350°F (175°C) oven for about 1 hour until a wooden pick inserted in center comes out clean. Cuts into 16 slices.

Pictured on page 35.

NUTRITION GUIDE.	1 slice contains:	
	Energy	148 Calories (619 kJ)
	Cholesterol	27 mg
	Sodium	175 mg
	Fat	4 g

REUBEN SANDWICH

A yummy fried corned beef and sauerkraut sandwich.

Rye bread slices	2	2
Prepared mustard	1 tsp.	5 mL
Thinly sliced corned beef	1 oz.	28 g
Sauerkraut, rinsed and drained	2 tbsp.	30 mL
Process skim mozzarella cheese slice (7% MF)	1	1
Margarine	1½ tsp.	7 mL

Spread 1 bread slice with mustard. Lay corned beef over top. Spread sauerkraut over corned beef followed by cheese and second bread slice.

Spread both outsides of sandwich with margarine. Spray hot frying pan with no-stick cooking spray. Add sandwich. Brown both sides. Cut diagonally. Serves 1.

NUTRITION GUIDE	1 sandwich contains:	
	Energy	317 Calories (1326 kJ)
	Cholesterol	27 mg
	Sodium	860 mg
	Fat	14 g

RICE MUFFINS

Flavorful and light.

Egg whites (large), room temperature	2	2
Leftover cooked rice	1 cup	250 mL
Egg yolk (large)	1	1
Vegetable cooking oil	2 tbsp.	30 mL
Skim milk	1 cup	250 mL
Salt	1/4 tsp.	1 mL
All-purpose flour	1 cup	250 mL

In small mixing bowl beat egg whites until stiff.

In another bowl using same beaters, beat rice, egg yolk, cooking oil, skim milk and salt.

Add flour. Stir. Fold in egg whites. Spray muffin cups with no-stick cooking spray. Fill cups. Bake in 400°F (205°C) oven for about 15 to 20 minutes. Serve warm. Makes 12 medium muffins.

Pictured on page 35.

NUTRITION GUIDE	1 muffin contains:	
	Energy	99 Calories (415 kJ)
	Cholesterol	18 mg
	Sodium	77 mg
	Fat	3 g

COTTAGE CHEESE MUFFINS

Moist and simply delicious.

All-purpose flour	1 1/2 cups	350 mL
Baking powder	1/2 tsp.	2 mL
Baking soda	1/2 tsp.	2 mL
Salt	1/2 tsp.	2 mL
Margarine, softened	1/4 cup	60 mL
Brown sugar, packed	3/4 cup	175 mL
Large egg	1	1
Low-fat cottage cheese (less than 1% MF)	1 cup	225 mL
Skim milk	1/4 cup	60 mL
Raisins or currants	1/2 cup	125 mL

(continued on next page)

Combine first 4 ingredients in bowl. Stir. Set aside.

Cream margarine and sugar in mixing bowl. Beat in egg. Add cottage cheese and milk. Beat to mix thoroughly.

Stir in raisins. Add flour mixture. Stir just to moisten. Spray muffin cups with no-stick cooking spray. Fill ³/₄ full. Bake in 375°F (190°C) oven for about 20 minutes. Makes 12 medium muffins.

Pictured on page 35.

NUTRITION GUIDE	1 muffin contains:	
	Energy	190 Calories (796 kJ)
	Cholesterol	19 mg
	Sodium	312 mg
	Fat	5 g

ONION MELT

If you have never had cheese and onion together, you are in for a treat. Top with two slices of cheese for more of a treat yet.

Sliced onion	**1¹/₃ cups**	**300 mL**
Cold water, lots		
Boiling water		
Bread slices, toasted	**4**	**4**
Process skim mozzarella cheese slices (7% MF)	**4**	**4**
Paprika, sprinkle		

Soak onion in cold water for 30 minutes. Drain.

Put onion into saucepan. Add boiling water. Bring to a boil. Simmer covered until tender. Drain.

Divide onion among toast slices. Lay 1 slice cheese over top of each. Sprinkle with paprika. Broil until cheese melts and browns a bit. Makes 4 servings.

NUTRITION GUIDE	1 serving contains:	
	Energy	158 Calories (661 kJ)
	Cholesterol	0 mg
	Sodium	143 mg
	Fat	3 g

MUFFINS

A plain muffin that is especially good for meals or snacks.

All-purpose flour	1³/₄ cups	400 mL
Granulated sugar	2 tbsp.	30 mL
Baking powder	1 tsp.	5 mL
Baking soda	¹/₂ tsp.	2 mL
Salt	¹/₂ tsp.	2 mL
Large egg	1	1
Buttermilk	1 cup	225 mL
Margarine, melted	2 tbsp.	30 mL

Sift first 5 ingredients into bowl. Make a well in center.

In small bowl beat egg until smooth. Add buttermilk and margarine. Pour into well. Stir just to moisten. Spray muffin cups with no-stick cooking spray. Fill cups ³/₄ full. Bake in 400°F (205°C) oven 15 to 20 minutes. Test with wooden pick. Makes 12 medium muffins.

NUTRITION GUIDE	1 muffin contains:	
	Energy	110 Calories (460 kJ)
	Cholesterol	19 mg
	Sodium	221 mg
	Fat	3 g

BRAN MUFFINS

Start your day with one of these. Uses sour milk.

Margarine, softened	¹/₂ cup	125 mL
Brown sugar, packed	²/₃ cup	150 mL
Large egg	1	1
Sour skim milk (1 tbsp., 15 mL, vinegar plus milk)	1 cup	250 mL
All-purpose flour	1²/₃ cups	375 mL
All bran cereal	1 cup	250 mL
Baking powder	1¹/₂ tsp.	7 mL
Baking soda	³/₄ tsp.	4 mL
Salt	¹/₄ tsp.	1 mL

(continued on next page)

Cream margarine and brown sugar together in mixing bowl. Beat in egg. Slowly mix in sour milk.

Measure remaining ingredients into a separate bowl. Stir well. Add to wet mixture in mixing bowl. Stir just to moisten. Spray muffin cups with no-stick cooking spray. Fill ³/₄ full with batter. Bake in 400°F (205°C) oven for 15 to 20 minutes. Makes 12 medium muffins.

Pictured on page 35.

NUTRITION GUIDE	1 muffin contains:	
	Energy	211 Calories (883 kJ)
	Cholesterol	18 mg
	Sodium	305 mg
	Fat	8 g

TOASTED HAM AND CHEESE

Always popular, with warm cheese oozing from the sandwich.

Whole wheat bread slices (100%)	2	2
Prepared mustard	1 tsp.	5 mL
Sweet pickle relish	1¹/₂ tsp.	7 mL
Thin slice of lean ham (1 oz., 28 g)	1	1
Process skim mozzarella cheese	1	1
slice (7% MF)		
Margarine	1¹/₂ tsp.	7 mL

Lay bread slices on working surface. Spread 1 slice with mustard and other slice with relish. Lay ham and cheese on 1 slice. Cover with second slice.

Spread both outside slices with margarine. Coat frying pan with no-stick cooking spray. Place sandwich in hot pan. Brown on both sides. Cut in half diagonally. Serves 1.

NUTRITION GUIDE	1 sandwich contains:	
	Energy	307 Calories (1284 kJ)
	Cholesterol	18 mg
	Sodium	982 mg
	Fat	11 g

VEGETARIAN SANDWICH

Nice and thick and appetizing. Full of stuff.

Whole wheat bread slices (100%)	2	2
Margarine	1½ tsp.	7 mL
Tomato slices	2	2
Peeled, sliced cucumber	¼ cup	60 mL
Pepper, sprinkle		
Grated carrot	2 tbsp.	30 mL
Alfalfa sprouts or bean sprouts	¼ cup	60 mL
Lettuce leaves	2	2
Light salad dressing (or mayonnaise)	1 tsp.	5 mL

Spread bread with margarine. On 1 slice, layer tomato, cucumber, pepper, carrot, alfalfa sprouts and lettuce. Spread second bread slice with salad dressing and place over top. Cut in half diagonally. Serves 1.

Pictured on page 35.

NUTRITION GUIDE	1 sandwich contains:	
	Energy	225 Calories (941 kJ)
	Cholesterol	2 mg
	Sodium	417 mg
	Fat	9 g

TOMATO CHEESE SANDWICH

A red and white lunch. Very good.

Whole wheat bread slices (100%)	2	2
Margarine	1½ tsp.	7 mL
Process skim mozzarella cheese slice (7% MF)	1	1
Tomato slices	2	2
Alfalfa sprouts	¼ cup	50 mL
Lettuce leaves	2	2
Light salad dressing (or mayonnaise)	1½ tsp.	7 mL

(continued on next page)

Spread bread slices with margarine.

Layer next 4 ingredients in order given on 1 slice.

Spread other slice with salad dressing. Place over filling. Cut sandwich in half diagonally. Serves 1.

NUTRITION GUIDE	1 sandwich contains:	
	Energy	286 Calories (992 kJ)
	Cholesterol	2 mg
	Sodium	434 mg
	Fat	11 g

SCOTCH SCONES

Fresh, hot biscuits for a meal or a snack are welcome anytime.

All-purpose flour	**2 cups**	**450 mL**
Baking soda	**1 tsp.**	**5 mL**
Cream of tartar	**1 tsp.**	**5 mL**
Granulated sugar	**2 tbsp.**	**30 mL**
Salt	**¹/₄ tsp.**	**1 mL**
Margarine	**2 tbsp.**	**30 mL**
Sour skim milk (1 tbsp., 15 mL, vinegar plus milk)	**³/₄ cup**	**175 mL**

Measure first 6 ingredients into bowl. Cut in margarine until crumbly.

Add sour milk. Stir just until a soft ball forms. Divide into 4 equal balls. Now divide each ball into 4 pieces. Arrange on ungreased baking sheet. Bake in 425°F (220°C) oven for about 10 to 15 minutes until risen and browned. Makes 16 scones.

Pictured on page 125.

NUTRITION GUIDE	1 scone contains:	
	Energy	84 Calories (351 kJ)
	Cholesterol	trace
	Sodium	175 mg
	Fat	2 g

BLUEBERRY MUFFINS

Make this with or without sugar. Using sugar makes them a bit more tender.

All-purpose flour	2 cups	500 mL
Baking powder	1 tsp.	5 mL
Baking soda	1 tsp.	5 mL
Finely grated lemon rind	1 tsp.	5 mL
Low-fat plain yogurt (less than 1% MF)	1 cup	250 mL
Liquid sweetener (see Note)	3$\frac{1}{4}$ tsp.	16 mL
Skim milk	$\frac{1}{2}$ cup	125 mL
Large egg, fork beaten	1	1
Blueberries, fresh or frozen	1 cup	250 mL

Mix first 4 ingredients in mixing bowl. Make a well in center.

Add yogurt, sweetener, lemon rind, milk and egg to well. Stir just until moistened.

Quickly stir in blueberries. Spray muffin cups with no-stick cooking spray. Fill ¾ full. Bake in 400°F (205°C) oven for about 15 to 20 minutes until golden. Yield: 12 medium muffins.

Pictured on page 35.

NUTRITION GUIDE	1 muffin contains:	
	Energy	109 Calories (456 kJ)
	Cholesterol	19 mg
	Sodium	143 mg
	Fat	trace

Note: To use sugar, omit sweetener and add ⅓ cup (75 mL) granulated sugar. Add 22 calories per muffin.

Please make less noise. If you want to whistle while you work, be a traffic policeman.

CHOCOLATE CHEESECAKE

This chilled cheesecake fills the craving for chocolate. It is creamy and has a lot of height to it. Decorate with whipped topping and raspberries.

CRUST

Margarine	2 tbsp.	30 mL
Chocolate wafer crumbs	²/₃ cup	150 mL

FILLING

Envelopes dessert topping	2	2
Skim milk	1 cup	225 mL
Unflavored gelatin	2 x ¹/₄ oz.	2 x 7g
Water	¹/₂ cup	125 mL
Cocoa	¹/₂ cup	125 mL
Low-fat cream cheese (less than 20% MF), softened	8 oz.	250
Low-fat cottage cheese (less than 1% MF), smoothed in blender or sieved	1 cup	225 mL
Liquid sweetener	3 tbsp.	45 mL
Vanilla	1 tsp.	5 mL
Chocolate wafer crumbs	1 tbsp.	15 mL

Crust: Melt margarine in small saucepan. Stir in wafer crumbs. Press in bottom of 8 inch (20 cm) springform pan. Chill.

Filling: Combine dessert topping and milk according to package directions. Beat until stiff. Set aside.

Sprinkle gelatin over water in small saucepan. Let stand 1 minute. Heat and stir to dissolve gelatin. Remove from heat.

Add cocoa. Whisk to blend. Cool to room temperature.

Beat cream cheese, smoothed cottage cheese, sweetener and vanilla together in mixing bowl until smooth. Add cocoa mixture. Beat slowly to mix. Fold in whipped topping. Pour into prepared pan. Smooth top.

Sprinkle with wafer crumbs. Chill. Makes 12 servings.

Pictured on cover.

NUTRITION GUIDE	**1 serving contains:**	
	Energy	173 Calories (722 kJ)
	Cholesterol	13 mg
	Sodium	286 mg
	Fat	8 g

Desserts - 33 - 62

RUMMY MELON

You probably never will find so light or so refreshing a dessert as this. A good hot day picker-upper!

Water	¼ cup	60 mL
Lemon juice	1 tbsp.	15 mL
Lime juice	1 tbsp.	15 mL
Rum flavoring	1 tsp.	5 mL
Liquid sweetener	1 tbsp.	15 mL
Cubed watermelon (or pineapple)	5 cups	1.13 L

Stir first 5 ingredients together in small bowl.

Put watermelon into medium bowl. Drizzle juice over top. Toss to coat. Chill for about 3 hours. Stir fruit 2 to 3 times during chilling. Makes 4 servings.

NUTRITION GUIDE	1 serving contains:	
	Energy	73 Calories (306 kJ)
	Cholesterol	0 mg
	Sodium	4 mg
	Fat	1 g

CHOCOLATE ORANGE CHEESECAKE

Soft as velvet with an orange sauce spooned around each wedge.

Semi-sweet chocolate baking squares	3 × 1 oz.	3 × 28 g
Frozen concentrated orange juice, unsweetened	1/3 cup	75 mL
Envelopes dessert topping	2	2
Skim milk	1 cup	225 mL

ORANGE SAUCE

Frozen concentrated orange juice, unsweetened	1/3 cup	75 mL
Water	1 cup	225 mL
Lemon juice	1 tbsp.	15 mL
Cornstarch	4 tsp.	20 mL
Liquid sweetener	1 tsp.	5 mL

TOPPING

Envelope dessert topping	1	1
Skim milk	1/2 cup	110 mL
Vanilla	1/2 tsp.	2 mL
Canned mandarin orange segments, drained	10 oz.	284 mL

Melt chocolate in orange juice in small saucepan over low heat. Stir often. Cool.

Beat topping and milk in small mixing bowl until stiff as package directions indicate. Fold in cooled chocolate mixture. Pour into 8 inch (20 cm) springform pan. Be sure to freeze at least 4 hours before serving.

Orange Sauce: Combine orange juice, water, lemon juice and cornstarch in small saucepan. Mix well. Heat and stir until it boils and thickens. Stir in sweetener. Cool. Makes 1 1/4 cups (275 mL).

Topping: Beat topping, milk and vanilla in small mixing bowl according to package directions. Put dollop on top of each piece.

Spoon sauce beside each wedge of cake on plate. Garnish with orange segments. Serves 12.

NUTRITION GUIDE	1 serving contains:	
	Energy	145 Calories (607 kJ)
	Cholesterol	trace
	Sodium	31 mg
	Fat	7 g

STRAWBERRY CRÊPES

These crêpes are lined with chocolate and fresh strawberries. Add whipped topping and a drizzle of melted chocolate for the final touch.

CRÊPES

Large egg	1	1
Skim milk	1/4 cup	60 mL
Water	1/3 cup	75 mL
All-purpose flour	2/3 cup	150 mL
Vegetable cooking oil	1 tbsp.	15 mL
Granulated sugar	1/4 tsp.	1 mL
Salt	1/16 tsp.	0.5 mL

FILLING

Semisweet chocolate chips	1/2 cup	125 mL
Thinly sliced fresh strawberries	1 cup	225 mL
Liquid sweetener	1/2 tsp.	2 mL
Frozen whipped topping, thawed	3/4 cup	175 mL
Semi-sweet chocolate chips, melted	2 tbsp.	30 mL

Crêpes: Beat egg in small bowl until frothy. Add remaining ingredients. Beat until smooth. Spoon about 2 tbsp. (30 mL) into heated pan. Use teflon coated pan, or spray other type pan with no-stick cooking spray. Tip pan in circular motion to spread thinly and evenly. Brown lightly on 1 side only. Cool. Makes 8 crêpes 5 inch (12.5 cm) diameter.

Filling: Melt first amount of chocolate chips in small saucepan over very low heat stirring often. Spread quickly over light colored side of crêpes.

Lightly stir strawberries and sweetener together in small bowl.

Place sliced strawberries, overlapping a bit, down center of crêpes. Roll. Pipe whipped topping over crêpes. Drizzle with second amount of chocolate. Makes 8 crêpes. Single serving is 2 crêpes. Serves 4.

Pictured on page 53.

NUTRITION GUIDE	1 crêpe contains:	
	Energy	111 Calories (464 kJ)
	Cholesterol	27 mg
	Sodium	35 mg
	Fat	5 g

LEMON CHEESECAKE

A chilled dessert containing no sugar. A light finish to a meal.

CRUST

Margarine	3 tbsp.	50 mL
Graham cracker crumbs	¾ cup	175 mL

FILLING

Unflavored gelatin	2 × ¼ oz.	2 × 7 g
Water	½ cup	125 mL
Low-fat cottage cheese (less than 1% MF), smoothed in blender or sieved	2 cups	450 mL
Low-fat plain yogurt (less than 1% MF)	1 cup	225 mL
Lemon juice	¼ cup	60 mL
Grated lemon rind	1 tsp.	5 mL
Liquid sweetener	2 tbsp.	30 mL
Frozen whipped topping, thawed	1 cup	225 mL

Crust: Melt margarine in small saucepan. Stir in crumbs. Press evenly into 8 inch (20 cm) springform pan. Chill.

Filling: Sprinkle gelatin over water in small saucepan. Let stand 1 minute. Heat and stir to dissolve gelatin. Cool. Don't chill.

Combine next 5 ingredients in bowl. Add cooled gelatin mixture. Chill until syrupy.

Fold in whipped topping. Spread over crust. Chill for 3 to 4 hours. Makes 10 servings.

NUTRITION GUIDE	1 serving contains:	
	Energy	144 Calories (601 kJ)
	Cholesterol	3 mg
	Sodium	319 mg
	Fat	7 g

CHOCOLATE PUDDING

Both the chocolate and vanilla puddings have good flavor. If you like, a dash of salt may be added.

Skim milk	1½ cups	350 mL
Cornstarch	3 tbsp.	50 mL
Cocoa	3 tbsp.	50 mL
Skim milk	½ cup	125 mL
Vanilla	1 tsp.	5 mL
Liquid sweetener, or to taste	2½ tsp.	12 mL

Heat first amount of milk in saucepan until it boils.

Meanwhile, mix cornstarch, cocoa and second amount of milk until smooth. Stir into boiling milk until it returns to a boil and thickens. Remove from heat.

Add vanilla and sweetener. Makes 2 cups (450 mL).

NUTRITION GUIDE	½ cup/125 mL contains:	
	Energy	85 Calories (357 kJ)
	Cholesterol	2 mg
	Sodium	68 mg
	Fat	1 g

VANILLA PUDDING: Simply omit cocoa.

FESTIVE FRUIT

A perfect ending for a big meal. Pierce each piece of fruit with a fork, dip and enjoy.

Slices of Banana Loaf, see page 24	6	6
Small cantaloupe	½	½
Pineapple pieces, fresh or canned	24	24
Fresh strawberries, halved	12	12
Fresh raspberries	36	36
Blueberries, fresh or frozen	36	36
Low-fat blueberry yogurt (less than 1% MF), or strawberry or raspberry	¾ cup	175 mL

(continued on next page)

Cut banana loaf slices in half crosswise. Overlap on side of each of 6 plates.

Cut slices of cantaloupe a generous ¹/₂ inch (12 mm) thick with blunt ends. Slice quite thin into 4 slices leaving slices joined at 1 end. Spread slightly and place on plate.

Arrange 4 pieces of pineapple on plate. Top each with ¹/₂ strawberry cut side down. Scatter 6 raspberries and 6 blueberries in center. Repeat for other 5 plates.

Spoon 2 tbsp. (30 mL) yogurt into small containers on plates or spoon directly onto plates. Serves 6.

Pictured on page 35.

NUTRITION GUIDE	1 serving contains:	
	Energy	219 Calories (918 kJ)
	Cholesterol	28 mg
	Sodium	207 mg
	Fat	4 g

RED FRUIT DESSERT

Rhubarb and strawberries combine to make this delicious sauce with no sugar added. Good over cake, ice milk, yogurt or just as a fruit dessert.

Rhubarb, in short lengths	**7¹/₂ cups**	**1.7 L**
Sliced fresh strawberries	**1 cup**	**250 mL**
Water	**¹/₃ cup**	**75 mL**
Liquid sweetener	**3¹/₂ tbsp.**	**50 mL**

Combine rhubarb, strawberries and water in medium saucepan. Bring to a boil. Cover and simmer slowly until tender. Remove from heat and cool.

Turn into serving bowl. Stir in sweetener. Makes 7 cups (1.6 L).

NUTRITION GUIDE	¹/₂ cup/125 mL contains:	
	Energy	18 Calories (74 kJ)
	Cholesterol	0 mg
	Sodium	3 mg
	Fat	trace

LEMON PUDDING

A light and satisfying dessert.

Egg whites (large), room temperature	2	2
Margarine, softened	$^{1}/_{4}$ **cup**	60 mL
Lemon juice	**2 tbsp.**	30 mL
Finely grated lemon rind	**1 tsp.**	5 mL
All-purpose flour	$^{3}/_{4}$ **cup**	175 mL
Granulated sugar	$^{1}/_{2}$ **cup**	125 mL
Skim milk	**1 cup**	225 mL
Lemon flavoring	$^{1}/_{4}$ **tsp.**	1 mL

Beat egg whites in small mixing bowl until stiff. Set aside.

Measure remaining ingredients into another bowl. Using same beaters beat until smooth. Fold in egg whites. Turn into 1 quart (1 L) casserole which has been coated with no-stick cooking spray. Bake in 350°F (175°C) oven for about 40 to 45 minutes until golden and barely firm. Serve warm. Makes $2^{2}/_{3}$ cups (600 mL) or 5 servings.

NUTRITION GUIDE	1 serving contains:	
	Energy	261 Calories (1091 kJ)
	Cholesterol	1 mg
	Sodium	155 mg
	Fat	9 g

One of life's biggest shocks when you first begin employment is how much your boss seems to share so many opinions of your parents.

Serve warm or cool with or without whipped topping.

Granulated sugar	⅓ cup	75 mL
All-purpose flour	1½ oupo	375 mL
Baking powder	1½ tsp.	7 mL
Baking soda	¾ tsp.	4 mL
Salt	¼ tsp.	1 mL
Ginger	1¼ tsp.	6 mL
Cinnamon	1 tsp.	5 mL
Buttermilk	½ cup	125 mL
Molasses	½ cup	125 mL
Margarine, softened	¼ cup	60 mL
Egg whites (large)	2	2

Measure first 7 ingredients into mixing bowl. Stir. Make a well in center.

Add remaining ingredients to well. Beat until smooth. Pour into 9 x 9 inch (22 x 22 cm) cake pan that has been coated with no-stick cooking spray. Bake in 350°F (175°C) oven for about 25 minutes until an inserted wooden pick comes out clean. Cut into 12 pieces.

NUTRITION GUIDE	1 piece contains:	
	Energy	159 Calories (666 kJ)
	Cholesterol	trace
	Sodium	215 mg
	Fat	4 g

If a locomotive could catch a cold, it would be Ah-choo-choo train.

VANILLA ICE CREAM

À la mode your desserts. Practically cholesterol free. You will want to double or triple the recipe after you try it.

Evaporated skim milk	1cup	225 mL
Corn starch	2 tsp.	10 mL
Granulated sugar	1/2 cup	110 mL
Salt, just a pinch		
Envelope of dessert topping	1	1
Skim milk	1/2 cup	110 mL
Vanilla	2 tsp.	10 mL

Whisk first 4 ingredients together in small saucepan. Heat and stir until it boils and thickens. Cool to room temperature.

Beat dessert topping and skim milk as package directs until stiff. Beat in vanilla. Fold into milk mixture. Pour into shallow 8 x 8 inch (20 x 20 cm) pan. Freeze. Makes about 2¼ cups (525 mL).

Pictured on page 53.

NUTRITION GUIDE	1/4 cup/60 mL contains:	
	Energy	106 Calories (444 kJ)
	Cholesterol	1 mg
	Sodium	48 mg
	Fat	2 g

GRAHAM WAFERS

So crispy and crunchy. Does not contain eggs.

Margarine, softened	1/2 cup	125 mL
Granulated sugar	1 cup	225 mL
Vanilla	1/2 tsp.	2 mL
Graham flour (see Note)	2 cups	450 mL
All-purpose flour	1 cup	225 mL
Baking powder	1/2 tsp.	2 mL
Baking soda	1/2 tsp.	2 mL
Salt	1/2 tsp.	2 mL
Skim milk	1/2 cup	125 mL

(continued on next page)

Cream margarine, sugar and vanilla.

Add next 5 ingredients. Beat on low or stir with spoon until crumbly.

Add milk. Mix in. Roll paper thin on lightly floured surface. Use a ruler for even cutting. Cut into 2¹/₂ inch (6.5 cm) squares. Arrange on ungreased baking sheets. No need to leave room for expansion. Prick evenly with fork. Bake in 350°F (175°C) oven for about 10 to 12 minutes until lightly browned. Remove from baking sheet while hot. Makes 6 dozen.

NUTRITION GUIDE	1 wafer contains:	
	Energy	42 Calories (175 kJ)
	Cholesterol	trace
	Sodium	44 mg
	Fat	1 g

Note: While graham flour is preferable, whole wheat flour may be used if necessary.

CHEESY ICING

Just meant for carrot cake although any cake would be enhanced when iced with this. Sugar free.

Dry curd unsalted cottage cheese (less than 1% MF)	**1 cup**	**225 mL**
Margarine, softened	**¹/₄ cup**	**60 mL**
Liquid sweetener	**4 tsp.**	**20 mL**
Skim milk	**1-2 tsp.**	**5-10 mL**

Place first 3 ingredients in blender. Blend smooth. Add a bit of milk if needed to make spreading consistency. Makes ⁷/₈ cup (200 mL). Spread over Carrot Cake, page 47, or any other cake.

NUTRITION GUIDE	1tbsp./15 mL contains:	
	Energy	38 Calories (160 kJ)
	Cholesterol	trace
	Sodium	39 mg
	Fat	3 g

PASTRY

Makes a tender low-fat crust.

All-purpose flour	**1 cup**	**250 mL**
Unsaturated cooking oil	**¼ cup**	**60 mL**
Water	**2 tbsp.**	**30 mL**
Salt	**¼ tsp.**	**1 mL**

Measure all 4 ingredients into bowl. Mix well. Roll between 2 sheets of waxed paper. Line 9 inch (22 cm) pie plate. Prick with fork. For recipe requiring baked pie shell, bake in 400°F (205°C) oven for about 10 minutes until browned. Cool and fill. For recipe requiring an unbaked shell, do not prick with fork. Fill shell. Bake on bottom rack as recipe directs. Makes one 9 inch (22 cm) pie shell. Serves 8.

NUTRITION GUIDE	⅛ **single crust contains:**	
	Energy	124 Calories (520 kJ)
	Cholesterol	0 mg
	Sodium	85 mg
	Fat	7 g

LOW-FAT PASTRY

Low fat and cholesterol free. Shrinkage is practically nil.

All-purpose flour	**1¾ cups**	**400 mL**
Vegetable shortening, softened	**6 tbsp.**	**100 mL**
Baking powder	**¼ tsp.**	**1 mL**
Water	**⅓ cup**	**75 mL**

Measure first 3 ingredients into bowl. Work together until crumbly.

Pour water all over top. Mix with fork then with your hands until it will hold together. You can roll this almost without flouring rolling surface. Roll thinly. Makes enough for 2 crusts. When baked this is quite firm but not tough. For a 2 crust pie, it is best to cut through top crust with a sharp knife while pie is still hot. Makes two 9 inch (22 cm) pie shells.

NUTRITION GUIDE	⅛ **single crust contains:**	
	Energy	95 Calories (401 kJ)
	Cholesterol	0 mg
	Sodium	1 mg
	Fat	5 g

Very tasty with a small amount of fat. Cheesy Icing, page 45, tops it off.

Vegetable cooking oil	¼ cup	60 mL
Granulated sugar	⅓ cup	75 mL
Large egg	1	1
Egg whites (large)	2	2
Crushed pineapple with juice, unsweetened	1 cup	250 mL
Vanilla	1 tsp.	5 mL
Finely grated carrot	1 cup	250 mL
Liquid sweetener	2 tsp.	10 mL
All-purpose flour	1½ cups	375 mL
Baking powder	1 tsp.	5 mL
Baking soda	1 tsp.	5 mL
Cinnamon	1 tsp.	5 mL
Nutmeg	⅛ tsp.	0.5 mL

Beat cooking oil, sugar, egg and egg whites together in mixing bowl. Stir in pineapple with juice, vanilla, carrot and liquid sweetener.

Add flour, baking powder, baking soda, cinnamon and nutmeg. Mix. Turn into 9 x 9 inch (22 x 22 cm) pan that has been sprayed with no-stick cooking spray. Bake in 350°F (175°C) oven for about 30 minutes until an inserted wooden pick comes out clean. Cool. Yield: 16 servings.

NUTRITION GUIDE	**1 serving contains:**	
	Energy	111 Calories (463 kJ)
	Cholesterol	14 mg
	Sodium	100 mg
	Fat	4 g

NO-SUGAR CARROT CAKE: Omit sugar. Add 4 tsp. (20 mL) liquid sweetener. Cake is not quite as tender but is quite acceptable.

One thing's certain, an octopus goes to battle well armed.

CHOCOLATE CAKE

A fine textured cake using just the whites from eggs. Dust with powdered sugar to serve or use a thin covering of chocolate icing.

All-purpose flour	**1¼ cups**	**275 mL**
Granulated sugar	**¾ cup**	**175 mL**
Cocoa	**¼ cup**	**60 mL**
Margarine, softened	**¼ cup**	**60 mL**
Baking powder	**1 tsp.**	**5 mL**
Baking soda	**1 tsp.**	**5 mL**
Salt	**¼ tsp.**	**1 mL**
Egg whites (large)	**2**	**2**
Vanilla	**1 tsp.**	**5 mL**
Hot water	**1 cup**	**225 mL**
Icing (confectioner's) sugar	**2 tsp.**	**10 mL**

Preheat oven to 350°F (175°C). Measure first 10 ingredients into mixing bowl in order given. Beat until smooth. Pour into 9 x 9 inch (22 x 22 cm) pan that has been sprayed with no-stick cooking spray. Bake in oven for about 30 to 35 minutes until an inserted wooden pick comes out clean.

Serve warm or cool. If serving cool, sift icing sugar over cake. Cut into 16 servings.

NUTRITION GUIDE	1 serving contains:	
	Energy	110 Calories (460 kJ)
	Cholesterol	0 mg
	Sodium	169 mg
	Fat	3 g

We have kept our teeth together much better with the invention of toothpaste.

So different. So pretty. Eat it out of hand. Try all sorts of fruits and toppings.

Fresh raspberries	²/₃ **cup**	**150 mL**
Fresh blueberries (or frozen, thawed)	¹/₃ **cup**	**75 mL**
Sliced strawberries	¹/₃ **cup**	**75 mL**
Low-fat cottage cheese (less than 1% MF)	¹/₄ **cup**	**60 mL**
Skim milk	**4 tsp.**	**20 mL**
Lemon juice	³/₄ **tsp.**	**4 mL**
Liquid sweetener	¹/₂ **tsp.**	**2 mL**
Flour tortillas, snack size (6 inch, 15 cm)	**8**	**8**

Combine fruit in shallow dish. Stir lightly to mix for easy dividing. Do not crush.

Run cottage cheese, milk, lemon juice and sweetener through blender.

Warm tortillas in covered container in 300°F (150°C) oven. They need to be warm so they won't break when folded. Fold in half then in half again. Lift 1 side to form a hollow. Spoon about 2¹/₂ tbsp. (37 mL) or about ¹/₈ fruit into hollow. Add about 1 tsp. (5 mL) of cottage cheese mixture and hold tortilla upright so it will run down through fruit. If too thick, a bit more milk may be added or fruit may be stirred into mixture before spooning into tortillas. Repeat. Makes 8. Single serving is 2.

Pictured on page 53.

<table>
<tr><td rowspan="5">N U T R I T I O N
G U I D E</td><td colspan="2">1 burrito contains:</td></tr>
<tr><td>Energy</td><td>107 Calories (445 kJ)</td></tr>
<tr><td>Cholesterol</td><td>trace</td></tr>
<tr><td>Sodium</td><td>135 mg</td></tr>
<tr><td>Fat</td><td>trace</td></tr>
</table>

Paré Pointer

Actually, a Yankee Doodle is simply an American drawing.

LIGHT FRUIT CAKE

Light in color as well as fruit. The addition of cherries and raisins makes it colorful. No eggs in this cake.

Margarine, softened	¼ cup	60 mL
Granulated sugar	½ cup	125 mL
Cinnamon	½ tsp.	2 mL
All-purpose flour	2 cups	450 mL
Sour skim milk (1 tbsp., 15 mL, vinegar plus milk)	1 cup	225 mL
Baking soda	1 tsp.	5 mL
Water	1 tsp.	5 mL
Candied cherries, halved	½ cup	125 mL
Raisins	½ cup	125 mL

Cream margarine, sugar and cinnamon together.

Add flour in 3 parts alternately with sour milk in 2 parts beginning and ending with flour.

Mix baking soda with water. Add. Stir.

Add cherries and raisins. Mix. Turn into 9 x 9 inch (22 x 22 cm) cake pan that has been sprayed with no-stick cooking spray. Bake in 375°F (190°C) oven for about 30 minutes until an inserted wooden pick comes out clean. Cut into 20 pieces.

NUTRITION GUIDE	1 piece contains:	
	Energy	121 Calories (505 kJ)
	Cholesterol	trace
	Sodium	102 mg
	Fat	2 g

Take your choice. Would you rather have laugh wrinkles or worry warts?

Good no-cholesterol pie without sugar. Sugar may be used instead of sweetener if desired. Use just a top crust if you want to slash fat grams in half.

Low-Fat Pastry, see page 46

Peeled and diced apples	**5 cups**	**1.12 L**
All-purpose flour	**2 tbsp.**	**30 mL**
Cinnamon	**¹/₂ tsp.**	**2 mL**
Liquid sweetener (see Note)	**2 tbsp.**	**30 mL**
Lemon juice	**1 tbsp.**	**15 mL**
Water (optional)	**1-4 tbsp.**	**15-60 mL**
Granulated sugar (optional)	**¹/₄-¹/₂ tsp.**	**1-2 mL**

Roll pastry and line 9 inch (22 cm) pie plate. Roll top crust.

Combine apple, flour and cinnamon in bowl. Toss to mix. Turn into pie shell.

In small cup mix sweetener, lemon juice and water. Drizzle over apple. If you prefer a juicier pie, add more water. Dampen pastry edges. Cover with top crust. Trim. Crimp to seal. Cut vents in top.

Sprinkle with sugar. Bake on bottom shelf in 350°F (175°C) oven about 45 minutes until apples are cooked and crust is browned. Serves 8.

Pictured on page 53.

NUTRITION GUIDE	**1 serving contains:**	
	Energy	249 Calories (1012 kJ)
	Cholesterol	0
	Sodium	1 mg
	Fat	10 g

Note: To use sugar rather than sweetener, omit water and sweetener. Add 1 cup (225 mL) granulated sugar. Add 102 calories per serving.

CHOCOLATE TRUFFLES

A real treat.

Low-fat cream cheese (less than 20% MF), softened	**6 oz.**	**187 g**
Liquid sweetener	**3 tbsp.**	**50 mL**
Vanilla	**1 tsp.**	**5 mL**
Graham cracker crumbs	**1³/₄ cups**	**400 mL**
Cocoa	**¹/₃ cup**	**75 mL**
Ground almonds	**¹/₄ cup**	**60 mL**

Combine cream cheese, sweetener and vanilla in bowl. Beat until mixed and smooth.

Add graham crumbs and cocoa. Mix. Shape into ³/₄ inch (2 cm) small balls.

Roll in ground almonds. Brush off crumbs a bit so they aren't too thick. Makes about 4¹/₂ dozen.

Pictured on page 53.

NUTRITION GUIDE	**1 truffle contains:**	
	Energy	27 Calories (113 kJ)
	Cholesterol	2 mg
	Sodium	48 mg
	Fat	1 g

FRUITY YOGURT PIE

A soft pink color with bits of strawberries showing. Very good. It will be difficult to convince guests that this is a low calorie dessert.

GRAHAM CRUMB CRUST

Margarine	1/3 cup	75 mL
Graham cracker crumbs	1 1/4 cups	275 mL
Liquid sweetener	1 1/2 tsp.	7 mL

FILLING

Low-fat plain yogurt (less than 1% MF)	1 cup	250 mL
Frozen whipped topping, thawed	2 cups	450 mL
Mashed fresh strawberries	1 cup	225 mL
Liquid sweetener	1 tsp.	5 mL

Graham Crumb Crust: Melt margarine in small saucepan. Stir in crumbs and sweetener. Press onto bottom and sides of 9 inch (22 cm) pie plate. Bake in 350°F (175°C) oven 10 to 12 minutes. Cool.

Filling: Fold yogurt and whipped topping together.

Stir mashed strawberries and liquid sweetener together. Fold into yogurt mixture. Pile into pie shell. Chill several hours. Makes 8 servings.

NUTRITION GUIDE	1 serving contains:	
	Energy	225 Calories (941 kJ)
	Cholesterol	1 mg
	Sodium	240 mg
	Fat	15 g

Paré Pointer

A neighbor fisherman advertised in the local newspaper for a fisher-woman. He promised her a reel good time.

GINGERSNAPS

Nicely rounded cookies, made without eggs.

Margarine, softened	**1 cup**	**225 mL**
Granulated sugar	**1 cup**	**225 mL**
Table molasses	**1 cup**	**225 mL**
Ginger	**1 tsp.**	**5 mL**
Baking soda	**1 tsp.**	**5 mL**
Salt	**¹/₂ tsp.**	**2 mL**
Boiling water	**¹/₂ cup**	**125 mL**
All-purpose flour	**4¹/₂ cups**	**1 L**

Beat margarine, sugar and molasses together in mixing bowl. Add ginger, baking soda and salt. Beat to mix. Slowly beat in boiling water until smooth.

Add flour. Stir until moistened. Roll pieces of dough into 1 inch (2.5 cm) balls. Arrange on ungreased baking sheet leaving space between each ball. Bake in 350°F (175°C) oven for about 12 minutes. Makes 7 dozen cookies.

Pictured on page 53.

N U T R I T I O N G U I D E	**1 cookie contains:**	
	Energy	64 Calories (269 kJ)
	Cholesterol	0 mg
	Sodium	58 mg
	Fat	2 g

CHOCOLATE MOUSSE

Tastes just like a diet wrecker. Dress it up with a dab of whipped topping if desired.

Skim milk powder	**1¹/₂ cups**	**350 mL**
Warm water	**6 tbsp.**	**90 mL**
Liquid sweetener	**¹/₂ tsp.**	**2 mL**
Instant chocolate pudding, 4 serving size	**1**	**1**
Cold water	**1 cup**	**225 mL**
Envelope dessert topping	**1**	**1**
Skim milk	**¹/₂ cup**	**110 mL**
Vanilla	**¹/₂ tsp.**	**2 mL**

(continued on next page)

Measure first 3 ingredients into blender. Process until smooth and thick.

Add pudding and cold water. Blend until smooth. Turn into bowl.

Beat dessert topping, skim milk and vanilla in small mixing bowl until stiff as package directs. Fold into chocolate mixture. Makes 4 cups (900 mL).

NUTRITION GUIDE	½ cup/125 mL contains:	
	Energy	141 Calories (592 kJ)
	Cholesterol	5 mg
	Sodium	222 mg
	Fat	2 g

COOKIE SNACKS

Eat your cookie and know the nutritional content when you do.

Margarine, softened	½ cup	125 mL
Brown sugar, packed	¾ cup	175 mL
Large egg	1	1
Vanilla	½ tsp.	2 mL
All-purpose flour	1¼ cups	275 mL
Baking soda	½ tsp.	2 mL
Salt	¼ tsp.	1 mL

Cream margarine and sugar together well in mixing bowl. Beat in egg and vanilla.

Add flour, baking soda and salt. Stir. Drop by rounded teaspoon onto cookie sheet that has been sprayed with no-stick cooking spray. Bake in 350°F (175°C) oven for about 12 to 14 minutes until firm. Makes 26 cookies.

Pictured on page 53.

NUTRITION GUIDE	1 cookie contains:	
	Energy	82 Calories (344 kJ)
	Cholesterol	8 mg
	Sodium	97 mg
	Fat	4 g

QUICK PUDDING

No eggs in this cakey pudding with a butterscotch sauce.

All-purpose flour	1 cup	250 mL
Brown sugar	1/3 cup	75 mL
Margarine, softened	2 tbsp.	30 mL
Baking powder	2 tsp.	10 mL
Salt	1/8 tsp.	0.5 mL
Raisins	1/3 cup	75 mL
Skim milk	1/2 cup	125 mL
Hot water	1 3/4 cups	400 mL
Cinnamon	1/2 tsp.	2 mL
Vanilla	1 tsp.	5 mL
Brown sugar, packed	2/3 cup	150 mL

Measure first 6 ingredients into mixing bowl. Stir. Add milk. Mix. Turn into 2 quart (2 L) casserole. Smooth top.

In same bowl combine remaining 4 ingredients. Stir. Pour carefully over top of batter. Do not stir. Bake, uncovered, in 350°F (175°C) oven for about 30 minutes. Serve hot. Makes 6 servings.

N U T R I T I O N G U I D E	1 serving contains:	
	Energy	295 Calories (1233 kJ)
	Cholesterol	trace
	Sodium	131 mg
	Fat	4 g

WHITE CAKE

There are no egg yolks in this cake. Good flavor and fine texture.

Egg whites (large), room temperature	3	3
Margarine, softened	6 tbsp.	90 mL
Granulated sugar	3/4 cup	175 mL
Skim milk	3/4 cup	175 mL
Vanilla	3/4 tsp.	4 mL
All-purpose flour	1 1/2 cup	350 mL
Baking powder	2 1/4 tsp.	11 mL
Salt	1/4 tsp.	1 mL

(continued on next page)

Beat egg whites in small mixing bowl until stiff. Set aside.

Using same beaters, beat margarine and sugar together. Slowly beat in milk and vanilla.

Add flour, baking powder and salt. Mix until moistened. Fold in egg whites. Turn into 9 x 9 inch (22 x 22 cm) pan that has been sprayed with no-stick cooking spray. Bake in 350°F (175°C) oven about 30 minutes, until an inserted wooden pick comes out clean. Cut into 16 pieces.

NUTRITION GUIDE	1 piece contains:	
	Energy	128 Calories (536 kJ)
	Cholesterol	trace
	Sodium	109 mg
	Fat	4 g

OATMEAL CRISPS

Cookies with a lighter touch.

Margarine, softened	¹/₂ **cup**	**125 mL**
Brown sugar, packed	³/₄ **cup**	**175 mL**
Large egg	**1**	**1**
Vanilla	**1 tsp.**	**5 mL**
Whole wheat flour	³/₄ **cup**	**175 mL**
Cinnamon	³/₄ **tsp.**	**4 mL**
Baking soda	¹/₂ **tsp.**	**2 mL**
Salt	¹/₄ **tsp.**	**1 mL**
Rolled oats	**1¹/₄ cups**	**275 mL**

Cream margarine and sugar together well. Beat in egg and vanilla.

Add flour, cinnamon, baking soda and salt. Stir to moisten.

Mix in rolled oats. Drop by rounded teaspoon onto cookie sheet that has been sprayed with no-stick cooking spray. Bake in 375°F (190°C) oven for about 10 minutes. Makes 34 cookies.

NUTRITION GUIDE	1 cookie contains:	
	Energy	67 Calories (281 kJ)
	Cholesterol	6 mg
	Sodium	75 mg
	Fat	3 g

RED BOTTOM PUDDING PIE

A cakey pie, tart but not sour. A whipped topping can be added.

Frozen whole raspberries, without sugar, thawed	**10 oz.**	**300 g**
Liquid sweetener	**1 tbsp.**	**15 mL**
Egg whites (large), room temperature	**2**	**2**
Margarine, softened	**3 tbsp.**	**50 mL**
Water	**6 tbsp.**	**100 mL**
Granulated sugar	**1/3 cup**	**75 mL**
All-purpose flour	**3/4 cup**	**175 mL**
Baking powder	**1 tsp.**	**5 mL**
Salt	**1/8 tsp.**	**0.5 mL**
Vanilla	**1/2 tsp.**	**2 mL**

Spread raspberries with their juice from thawing, in 9 inch (22 cm) foil or glass pie plate. Add sweetener. Stir to mix.

Beat egg whites in small mixing bowl until stiff. Set aside.

In another bowl beat margarine, water and sugar together. Stir in flour, baking powder, salt and vanilla. Fold in egg whites. Spoon over raspberries. Bake in 375°F (190°C) oven for about 25 to 30 minutes until an inserted wooden pick comes out clean, and top is lightly browned. Makes 8 servings.

Pictured on page 53.

NUTRITION GUIDE	**1 serving contains:**	
	Energy	139 Calories (582 kJ)
	Cholesterol	0 mg
	Sodium	107 mg
	Fat	4 g

That bank robber must be a tinsmith. Did you see he made a bolt for the door?

Excellent cake, not light, not dark. Has no eggs.

Raisins	2 cups	500 mL
Water	1 cup	250 mL
Brown sugar, packed	1 cup	250 mL
Margarine	1/3 cup	75 mL
Cinnamon	1 tsp.	5 mL
Cloves	1/4 tsp.	1 mL
Nutmeg	1/4 tsp.	1 mL
Baking soda	1 tsp.	5 mL
Water	1 tsp.	5 mL
All-purpose flour	2 cups	500 mL
Baking powder	1 tsp.	5 mL
Salt	1/4 tsp.	1 mL

Combine first 7 ingredients in saucepan. Heat, stirring occasionally, until it boils. Boil for 3 minutes. Remove from heat.

Stir baking soda into second amount of water. Add to saucepan. Stir.

Add flour, baking powder and salt. Mix. Turn into 9 x 5 inch (22 x 12 cm) loaf pan which has been coated with no-stick cooking spray. Bake in 350°F (175°C) oven for about 40 minutes until an inserted wooden pick comes out clean. Makes 14 servings.

NUTRITION GUIDE	1 serving contains:	
	Energy	237 Calories (992 kJ)
	Cholesterol	0 mg
	Sodium	208 mg
	Fat	5 g

Paré Pointer

Don't ever run over a bird when mowing the lawn. You could end up with shredded tweet.

STUFFED PEACHES

A terrific ending. The topping tastes like dessert even though it is cottage cheese.

Low-fat cottage cheese (less than 1% MF)	¹/₂ cup	125 mL
Liquid sweetener	¹/₄ tsp.	1 mL
Vanilla	¹/₈ tsp.	0.5 mL
Peach halves, fresh or unsweetened canned, drained	4	4
Margarine	1 tsp.	5 mL
Graham cracker crumbs	1 tbsp.	15 mL

Mix cottage cheese, liquid sweetener and vanilla. Mash with fork.

Spoon onto each peach half.

Melt margarine in small saucepan. Stir in graham crumbs. Sprinkle over cottage cheese. Makes 4 servings.

NUTRITION GUIDE	1 serving contains:	
	Energy	66 Calories (275 kJ)
	Cholesterol	1 mg
	Sodium	148 mg
	Fat	2 g

CURRY SAUCE

A sauce that is good on its own. Especially good to use if you want to keep from salting your meat. Use this instead, on broiled meat and fish.

Margarine	1 tbsp.	15 mL
Finely chopped onion	¹/₃ cup	75 mL
All-purpose flour	4 tsp.	20 mL
Curry powder	1 tsp.	5 mL
Pepper	¹/₈ tsp.	0.5 mL
Chicken bouillon packet (35% less salt)	1 × ¹/₄ oz.	1 × 6.5 g
Water	1¹/₄ cups	275 mL

(continued on next page)

Melt margarine in frying pan. Add onion. Sauté until soft.

Sprinkle flour, curry powder, pepper and bouillon powder over onion. Mix. Stir in water. Heat and stir until mixture boils and thickens. Strain. Makes ³/₄ cup (175 mL).

NUTRITION GUIDE	1 tbsp./15 mL contains:	
	Energy	15 Calories (63 kJ)
	Cholesterol	trace
	Sodium	96 mg
	Fat	1 g

PINEAPPLE TOPPING

Good for a dessert topping. Especially good served with ham.

Crushed pineapple with juice, unsweetened	**14 oz.**	**398 mL**
Water	**¹/₂ cup**	**125 mL**
Lemon juice	**1 tbsp.**	**15 mL**
Cornstarch	**2 tbsp.**	**30 mL**
Liquid sweetener	**1 tbsp.**	**15 mL**

Put first 4 ingredients into medium saucepan. Stir well to blend in cornstarch. Heat and stir until it boils and thickens. Remove from heat. Cool.

Stir in liquid sweetener adding more or less to taste. Makes 1³/₄ cups (400 mL).

NUTRITION GUIDE	1 tbsp./15 mL contains:	
	Energy	7 Calories (30 kJ)
	Cholesterol	0 mg
	Sodium	trace
	Fat	trace

PINEAPPLE RAISIN SAUCE: Add ¹/₄ cup (60 mL) raisins or currants. Simmer until raisins soften a bit. Serve over Gingerbread, page 43, or other cake or ham steaks, roast beef, pork, lamb or chicken. Makes 2 cups (450 mL).

CREAM CHEESE SUBSTITUTE

This looks like cream cheese and the taste is amazing.

**Low-fat cottage cheese, (less than 1% MF), 1 cup   225 mL
    rinsed and drained**
Margarine, softened   ¼ cup   60 mL

Drain cottage cheese well. Press against side of sieve if necessary. Place in blender along with margarine. Blend smooth. Store covered in refrigerator. Makes 1 cup (225 mL).

N U T R I T I O N G U I D E	**1 tbsp./15 mL contains:**	
	Energy	36 Calories (162 kJ)
	Cholesterol	1 mg
	Sodium	102 mg
	Fat	3 g

Note: Use in place of cream cheese in recipes not requiring cooking.

SEAFOOD COCKTAIL SAUCE

Good flavor. Perfect for shrimp and other seafood.

Tomato paste	**¼ cup**	**60 mL**
Light salad dressing (or mayonnaise)	**¼ cup**	**60 mL**
Skim milk	**¼ cup**	**60 mL**
Lemon juice	**1 tsp.**	**5 mL**
Worcestershire sauce	**½ tsp.**	**2 mL**
Prepared horseradish	**½ tsp.**	**2 mL**

Mix all 6 ingredients in small bowl. A little more horseradish may be used if you wish. Store in refrigerator. Makes ¾ cup (175 mL).

N U T R I T I O N G U I D E	**1 tbsp./15 mL contains:**	
	Energy	22 Calories (93 kJ)
	Cholesterol	trace
	Sodium	50 mg
	Fat	1 g

MOCK WHIPPED CREAM

This has a slight marshmallow consistency. Good holding power. An agreeable topping.

Unflavored gelatin	1 tsp.	5 mL
Water	1/4 cup	60 mL
Ice water	1/2 cup	125 mL
Skim milk powder	1/2 cup	125 mL
Vegetable cooking oil	3 tbsp.	45 mL
Liquid sweetener	2 1/4 tsp.	11 mL

Sprinkle gelatin over first amount of water in small saucepan. Let stand 1 minute. Heat and stir to dissolve gelatin. Cool, but don't let it set.

Beat ice water and milk powder in small cold mixing bowl until stiff peaks form. With beater running add gelatin mixture, cooking oil and sweetener. Put in freezer for 15 minutes. Transfer to refrigerator. When ready to use, stir lightly. Makes 4 cups (900 mL).

Pictured on page 53.

NUTRITION GUIDE	1/4 cup/60 mL contains:	
	Energy	38 Calories (159 kJ)
	Cholesterol	1 mg
	Sodium	21 mg
	Fat	3 g

MOCK SOUR CREAM

Only two ingredients are blended to make this acceptable sour cream.

Low-fat cottage cheese (less than 1% MF)	1 cup	225 mL
Low-fat plain yogurt (less than 1% MF)	2 tbsp.	30 mL

Run both ingredients through blender to smooth them. Makes about 1 cup (225 mL).

NUTRITION GUIDE	1 tbsp./15 mL contains:	
	Energy	12 Calories (51 kJ)
	Cholesterol	1 mg
	Sodium	64 mg
	Fat	trace

JELLY FRUIT DESSERT

Sparkling with fruit. A whipped topping makes this more special.

Unflavored gelatin	1 x ¹/₄ oz.	1 x 7 g
Water	¹/₄ cup	50 mL
Canned sugar-free fruit cocktail (juice reserved)	14 oz.	398 mL
Unsweetened raspberry flavored drink crystals	¹/₂ x ¹/₅ oz.	¹/₂ x 6 g
Reserved juice plus water to make	2 cups	450 mL
Liquid sweetener	2 tsp.	10 mL

Sprinkle gelatin over first amount of water in small saucepan. Let stand 1 minute. Heat and stir until gelatin dissolves. Remove from heat.

Drain fruit and reserve juice.

Combine drink crystals, reserved juice with water, and sweetener in bowl. Stir to dissolve drink crystals. Add gelatin and fruit. Stir. Chill until firm. If you want fruit throughout, stir occasionally as gelatin sets. Makes 6 servings.

N U T R I T I O N G U I D E	1 serving contains:	
	Energy	28 Calories (115 kJ)
	Cholesterol	0 mg
	Sodium	4 mg
	Fat	0 g

JELLIED BANANA DESSERT: Omit canned fruit. Add 2 medium bananas, sliced.

BEST MOCK SOUR CREAM

Use on baked potatoes and save a bundle on calories and fat. One of the good fakes.

Low-fat cottage cheese (less than 1% MF)	1 cup	225 mL
Skim milk	2 tbsp.	30 mL
Lemon juice	1 tbsp.	15 mL

(continued on next page)

Combine all 3 ingredients in blender. Blend until smooth. Makes about 1 cup (225 mL).

NUTRITION GUIDE	1 tbsp./15 mL contains:	
	Energy	12 Calories (51 kJ)
	Cholesterol	1 mg
	Sodium	64 mg
	Fat	trace

FLUFFY MOCK SOUR CREAM: Add an additional 3$\frac{1}{3}$ tbsp. (50 mL) skim milk to blender. Makes a thinner mixture. Add a bit of sweetener to taste. Use as a sauce over fresh fruit. Makes 1$\frac{1}{2}$ cups (350 mL).

BARBECUE SAUCE

A good tangy sauce.

Water	$\frac{2}{3}$ cup	150 mL
Tomato paste	$\frac{1}{3}$ cup	75 mL
Vinegar	$\frac{1}{4}$ cup	60 mL
Worcestershire sauce	1 tbsp.	15 mL
Cornstarch	1 tbsp.	15 mL
Liquid smoke	1 tsp.	5 mL
Liquid sweetener	1 tsp.	5 mL

Stir all 7 ingredients together in saucepan over medium heat until it boils and thickens. Use to baste barbecued meat during the last 5 to 10 minutes of cooking. May also be used to baste oven cooked meat during last 5 to 10 minutes of cooking. Makes 1$\frac{1}{4}$ cups (275 mL).

NUTRITION GUIDE	1 tbsp./15 mL contains:	
	Energy	6 Calories (26 kJ)
	Cholesterol	0 mg
	Sodium	12 mg
	Fat	trace

Note: If you want a thin sauce, omit cornstarch, in which case you also omit cooking step. Just stir ingredients together.

BANANA FLUFF TOPPING

This piles softly onto cakes. Dark creamy color with flecks of bananas showing.

Large ripe bananas, thinly sliced	2	2
Egg whites (large)	2	2
Vanilla	1 tsp.	5 mL
Liquid sweetener	³/₄ tsp.	4 mL

Put all 4 ingredients into small mixing bowl. Beat until light and fluffy. This will take about 4 to 5 minutes. Use as topping for cakes or fresh fruit. Makes 3 cups (675 mL).

NUTRITION GUIDE	1 tbsp./15 mL contains:	
	Energy	5 Calories (23 kJ)
	Cholesterol	0 mg
	Sodium	2 mg
	Fat	trace

WHIPPED CREAM SUBSTITUTE

This is closer to the real thing than most substitutes.

Ice cold water	¹/₂ cup	125 mL
Lemon juice	³/₄ tsp.	4 mL
Skim milk powder	¹/₂ cup	125 mL
Liquid sweetener	1¹/₂ tsp.	7 mL
Vanilla	¹/₂ tsp.	2 mL

Measure water and lemon juice into small mixing bowl. Add milk powder. Beat slowly to moisten then beat at high speed until stiff.

Beat in sweetener and vanilla. Use within 45 minutes of preparing. It doesn't hold well for a longer period. Makes 3¹/₄ cups (725 mL).

NUTRITION GUIDE	1 tbsp./15 mL contains:	
	Energy	5 Calories (19 kJ)
	Cholesterol	trace
	Sodium	7 mg
	Fat	trace

MUSTARD SAUCE

A partner meant for ham. Also delicious served with beef.

All-purpose flour	2 tbsp.	30 mL
Skim milk	³/₄ cup	175 mL
Skim milk powder	¹/₃ cup	75 mL
Prepared mustard	3¹/₂ tsp.	17 mL
Onion powder	¹/₄ tsp.	1 mL
Vinegar	4 tsp.	20 mL
Liquid sweetener	1 tsp.	5 mL
Salt	¹/₈ tsp.	0.5 mL

Mix flour with part of milk until smooth. Add rest of milk along with remaining ingredients. Heat and stir until mixture boils and thickens. Chill until needed. Use as a dipping sauce for meatballs or as a sauce to go over meat. Makes ³/₄ cup (175 mL).

NUTRITION GUIDE	1 tbsp./15 mL contains:	
	Energy	25 Calories (104 kJ)
	Cholesterol	1 mg
	Sodium	79 mg
	Fat	trace

SEASONING

Use as salt substitute.

Paprika	2 tbsp.	30 mL
Poultry seasoning	1 tsp.	5 mL
Garlic powder	1 tsp.	5 mL
Celery seed	1 tsp.	5 mL
Onion powder	³/₄ tsp.	4 mL
Curry powder	¹/₂ tsp.	2 mL

Measure all ingredients into blender. Blend smooth. Cover to store. Makes 3¹/₃ tbsp. (50 mL).

NUTRITION GUIDE	1 tsp./5 mL contains:	
	Energy	7 Calories (30 kJ)
	Cholesterol	0 mg
	Sodium	1 mg
	Fat	trace

STEAK FRY

Zip up plain steak with a good tangy mustard spread. Top with onion.

Vegetable cooking oil	2 tbsp.	30 mL
Spanish onions, thinly sliced	2	2
Pepper, sprinkle		
Dijon mustard	1½ tbsp.	25 mL
Low-fat sour cream (7% MF)	1½ tbsp.	25 mL
Chopped parsley	1½ tsp.	7 mL
Lean sirloin steak, cut in 4 portions	1 lb.	454 g

Heat cooking oil in frying pan. Add onion. Sauté until cooked, about 8 minutes. Sprinkle with pepper. Transfer to small bowl and keep warm.

In small cup stir mustard, sour cream and parsley.

Broil or fry steaks to doneness desired. Spread mustard mixture over each steak. Cover with onion. Makes 4 servings.

NUTRITION GUIDE	1 serving contains:	
	Energy	244 Calories (1020 kJ)
	Cholesterol	56 mg
	Sodium	154 mg
	Fat	12 g

1. Swiss Steak page 82
2. Stir-Fry Meal page 73
3. Green Pepper Steak page 74

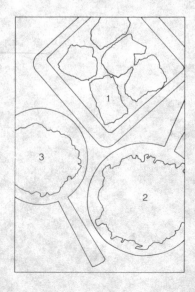

Simply delectable!

Vegetable cooking oil	1 tbsp.	15 mL
Chicken breast, halved, skin and bone removed	1	1
Bok choy or suey choy, torn up, packed	1 cup	250 mL
Sliced fresh mushrooms	1 cup	250 mL
Broccoli florets, cut small	1 cup	250 mL
Large handful fresh bean sprouts	1 cup	250 mL
Grated carrot	1 cup	250 mL
Red or green pepper, slivered	1	1
Frozen whole pea pods (or fresh)	6 oz.	170 g
Water	3 tbsp.	50 mL
Light soy sauce (40% less salt)	¼ cup	60 mL
Ginger	⅛ tsp.	0.5 mL
Garlic powder	⅛ tsp.	0.5 mL
Pepper	¼ tsp.	1 mL
Cornstarch	1 tsp.	5 mL

Heat cooking oil in wok or frying pan. Cut chicken into small pieces. Add chicken to wok or frying pan. Stir-fry until no pink remains. Transfer chicken to bowl.

Add next 7 ingredients to wok. Stir-fry about 3 minutes.

Add water. Stir in chicken. Cover and simmer approximately 7 minutes until cooked.

Mix remaining ingredients in small cup. Stir into vegetable mixture. Stir-fry to mix and thicken. Makes 2 servings.

Pictured on page 71.

NUTRITION GUIDE	**1 serving contains:**	
	Energy	307 Calories (1285 kJ)
	Cholesterol	69 mg
	Sodium	1462 mg
	Fat	9 g

GREEN PEPPER STEAK

Economical dish using round steak. A good make-ahead.

Vegetable cooking oil	2 tsp.	10 mL
Sirloin or round steak, boneless, cut in thin strips, all visible fat removed	1 lb.	454 g
Vegetable cooking oil	2 tsp.	10 mL
Green peppers, cut in strips	2	2
Medium onion, cut in strips	1	1
Sliced celery	1 cup	250 mL
Canned tomatoes	1 cup	250 mL
Garlic powder	1/4 tsp.	1 mL
Ginger	1/4 tsp.	1 mL
Beef bouillon packet (35% less salt)	1 x 1/4 oz.	1 x 6.5 g
Sliced, fresh mushrooms	2 cups	450 mL
Water	1/3 cup	75mL
Granulated sugar	1/4 tsp.	1 mL
Light soy sauce (40% less salt)	2 tsp.	10 mL
Sherry (or alcohol-free sherry)	1 tbsp.	15 mL

Heat first amount of cooking oil in frying pan. Add beef. Fry until browned well. Remove to 2 quart (2.5 L) casserole.

Add second amount of cooking oil to frying pan. Add green pepper, onion and celery. Sauté until onion is clear. Add to casserole.

Add next 9 ingredients to casserole. Cover. Cook in 350°F (175°C) oven for about 1 hour or more until meat is very tender. Makes 4 servings.

Pictured on page 71.

NUTRITION GUIDE	**1 serving contains:**	
	Energy	259 Calories (1084 kJ)
	Cholesterol	56 mg
	Sodium	458 mg
	Fat	11 g

A full bodied meat sauce covers a plateful of spaghetti. Add a salad for a complete meal.

TOMATO DEEF SAUCE

Lean ground beef	³/₄ lb.	342 g
Chopped onion	1 cup	225 mL
Chopped green pepper	¹/₃ cup	75 mL
Canned tomatoes	14 oz.	398 mL
Sliced, fresh mushrooms	2 cups	450 mL
Grated carrot	¹/₂ cup	125 mL
Granulated sugar	¹/₂ tsp.	2 mL
Vinegar	2 tsp.	10 mL
Worcestershire sauce	1 tsp.	5 mL
Oregano	¹/₂ tsp.	2 mL
Basil	¹/₂ tsp.	2 mL
Pepper	¹/₄ tsp.	1 mL
Frozen peas	1 cup	225 mL

SPAGHETTI

Spaghetti	8 oz.	250 g
Boiling water	3 qts.	4 L
Grated low-fat medium Cheddar cheese (less than 21% MF)	¹/₂ cup	125 mL

Tomato Beef Sauce: Sauté ground beef, onion and green pepper in frying pan sprayed with no-stick cooking spray until no pink remains in meat.

Add next 9 ingredients. Cover. Simmer slowly for about 15 minutes.

Add peas. Simmer about 3 minutes to cook. Makes 4¹/₈ cups (930 mL).

Spaghetti: In large, uncovered saucepan, cook spaghetti in boiling water until tender but firm, about 11 to 13 minutes. Drain. Divide among 4 dinner plates. Spoon sauce over top.

Sprinkle with cheese. Makes 4 servings.

Pictured on page 143.

NUTRITION GUIDE	**1 serving contains:**	
	Energy	527 Calories (2205 kJ)
	Cholesterol	56 mg
	Sodium	525 mg
	Fat	18 g

LEAN LOAF

A flavorful meat loaf with ground beef and cottage cheese. Very moist.

Lean ground beef	1 lb.	454 g
Low-fat cottage cheese (less than 1% MF), sieved	1 cup	225 mL
Egg whites (large)	2	2
All-purpose flour	2 tbsp.	30 mL
Parsley flakes	1/2 tsp.	2 mL
Onion powder	1/2 tsp.	2 mL
Pepper	1/4 tsp.	1 mL
Dry bread crumbs	1/2 cup	125 mL
Water	1/4 cup	60 mL
Ketchup	1 tbsp.	15 mL

In large bowl mix first 9 ingredients. Pack into small 4×8 inch (10×20 cm) loaf pan that has been sprayed with no-stick cooking spray.

Spread ketchup over top. Bake, uncovered, in 350°F (175°C) oven for about 1¼ hours. Cut into 10 slices. Single serving 2 slices.

NUTRITION GUIDE	2 slices contain:	
	Energy	299 Calories (1253 kJ)
	Cholesterol	53 mg
	Sodium	407 mg
	Fat	15 g

HAMBURGER CASSEROLE

So tasty with the flavor of cabbage rolls.

Long grain rice	1 cup	250 mL
Boiling water	2 cups	500 mL
Vegetable cooking oil	2 tbsp.	30 mL
Chopped onion	1 cup	250 mL
Lean ground beef	1 lb.	454 g
Pepper	1/8 tsp.	0.5 mL
Grated cabbage, packed	2 cups	500 mL

(continued on next page)

Canned tomatoes	**1 cup**	**250 mL**
Water	**½ cup**	**125 mL**
All-purpose flour	**2 tbsp.**	**30 mL**
Basil	**¼ tsp.**	**1 mL**
Salt	**¼ tsp.**	**1 mL**
Pepper	**¼ tsp.**	**1 mL**
Garlic powder	**¼ tsp.**	**1 mL**
Granulated sugar	**½ tsp.**	**2 mL**
Water	**¼ cup**	**60 mL**

Simmer rice in first amount of water in small covered saucepan for about 15 minutes until tender.

Heat cooking oil in frying pan. Add onion, ground beef and first amount of pepper. Scramble-fry until onion is soft and clear and no pink remains in meat. Add rice to meat mixture. Stir well. Turn into 3 quart (4 L) casserole.

Spread cabbage over top.

Heat tomatoes and second amount of water in saucepan until it boils.

Measure remaining 7 ingredients into cup. Mix until smooth. Stir into boiling liquid until it returns to a boil and thickens. Pour over casserole. Cover. Bake in 350°F (175°C) oven for about 1 hour until cabbage is cooked and casserole is bubbling hot. Makes 6 cups (1.35 L) or 6 servings.

NUTRITION GUIDE	**1 serving contains:**	
	Energy	360 Calories (1506 kJ)
	Cholesterol	43 mg
	Sodium	239 mg
	Fat	17 g

Paré Pointer

Equality has hit the sheep farmer. He will shear and shear alike.

MEAT PATTIES

These large patties are superb. Grated potato makes an excellent filler. A rich looking reddish sauce. A must-try.

Lean ground beef	³/₄ lb.	342 g
Grated potato	³/₄ cup	175 mL
Finely chopped onion	¹/₃ cup	75 mL
All-purpose flour	2 tbsp.	30 mL
Salt	¹/₄ tsp.	1 mL
Pepper	¹/₄ tsp.	1 mL
Tomato juice	1 cup	225 mL

Mix first 6 ingredients in bowl. Shape into 6 patties. Spray hot frying pan with no-stick cooking spray. Brown patties on both sides. The object is to brown the patties, not necessarily to cook them.

Pour tomato juice over meat. Cover. Simmer slowly for about 20 to 25 minutes. Check to see if liquid is absorbed. Add a bit of water if necessary. Arrange meat on serving plate. Spoon remaining sauce over top. Makes 6 servings.

NUTRITION GUIDE	1 meat patty contains:	
	Energy	159 Calories (666 kJ)
	Cholesterol	32 mg
	Sodium	303 mg
	Fat	9 g

BEEF BAKE

This is similar to scalloped potatoes but contains meat as a bonus. If on a sodium restricted diet, use low sodium canned soup in ingredients.

Sirloin steak, cubed	1¹/₄ lbs.	570 g
Chopped onion	1¹/₄ cups	275 mL
Vegetable cooking oil	1 tbsp.	15 mL
Sliced, fresh mushrooms	2 cups	450 mL
Water	²/₃ cup	150 mL

(continued on next page)

Medium potatoes, peeled, thinly sliced	3	3
Condensed cream of mushroom soup	10 oz.	284 mL
All-purpose flour	1½ tbsp.	25 mL
Skim milk	½ cup	125 mL
Low-fat plain yogurt (less than 1% MF)	½ cup	125 mL
Pepper	¼ tsp.	1 mL
Margarine	2 tbsp.	30 mL
Grated low-fat sharp Cheddar cheese (less than 21% MF)	½ cup	125 mL
Dry bread crumbs	½ cup	125 mL

Put meat and onion into pan with cooking oil. Brown well. Turn into medium saucepan.

Add mushrooms and water. Bring to a boil. Cover. Simmer about 1½ hours until meat is tender. Add more water if it gets dry. Turn into 3 quart (4 L) casserole.

Arrange potato slices over meat, overlapping slices.

Mix soup and flour well. Add milk, yogurt and pepper. Spoon over potato. Bake, covered, in 350°F (175°C) oven for 1 hour or until potatoes are tender.

Melt margarine in small saucepan. Stir in cheese and bread crumbs. Sprinkle over casserole. Return to oven. Bake, uncovered, about 20 minutes more until lightly browned. Makes 6 servings.

NUTRITION GUIDE	**1 serving contains:**	
	Energy	397 Calories (1661 kJ)
	Cholesterol	53 mg
	Sodium	777 mg
	Fat	18 g

Paré Pointer

In some countries elephants call each other on the elephone.

BEEF STROGANOFF

Rich brown color. A splendid dish.

Margarine	**1¹/₂ tbsp.**	**25 mL**
Beef fillet, cut postage stamp size, ¹/₄ inch (6 mm) thick	**1 lb.**	**454 g**
Margarine	**2 tsp.**	**10 mL**
Chopped onion	**1 cup**	**250 mL**
Fresh button mushrooms	**2 cups**	**450 mL**
All-purpose flour	**1¹/₂ tbsp.**	**25 mL**
Beef bouillon packets (35% less salt)	**2 × ¹/₄ oz.**	**2 × 6.5 g**
Boiling water	**1¹/₄ cups**	**275 mL**
Pepper	**¹/₈ tsp.**	**0.5 mL**
Paprika	**¹/₄ tsp.**	**1 mL**
Low-fat plain yogurt (less than 1 % MF)	**²/₃ cup**	**150 mL**

Heat first amount of margarine in frying pan. Add beef. Sauté to brown well. Cook to degree of doneness desired. Transfer meat to small bowl.

Add second amount of margarine to frying pan. Add onion and mushrooms. Sauté until soft.

Sprinkle with flour. Mix.

Dissolve bouillon powder in boiling water. Stir into onion mixture until it boils and thickens. Add pepper and paprika.

Add yogurt and meat. Stir and heat through. Makes 4 servings.

NUTRITION GUIDE	**1 serving contains:**	
	Energy	299 Calories (1251 kJ)
	Cholesterol	47 mg
	Sodium	463 mg
	Fat	15 g

CUBED STEAK

Once this economical steak is browned, simmered and combined with mushrooms, tender cubes are the result. To make a creamy sauce add a large spoonful of low-fat yogurt just before serving.

Round steak, cubed, all visible fat removed	1 lb.	454 g
Margarine	1 tbsp.	15 mL
Water	1½ cups	375 mL
Garlic powder	¼ tsp.	1 mL
Salt	¼ tsp.	1 mL
Pepper	¼ tsp.	1 mL
Sliced, fresh mushrooms	2 cups	450 mL
All-purpose flour	2 tbsp.	30 mL
Water	¼ cup	60 mL

Brown steak cubes in margarine in frying pan. Brown very well. Transfer meat to medium saucepan.

Pour first amount of water into frying pan. Loosen all brown bits. Pour over meat. Add garlic powder, salt and pepper. Bring to a boil. Simmer, covered, about 1 hour until tender.

Add mushrooms. Cook for another ½ hour until meat is very tender. Drain and measure juice. Add water to make 2 cups (450 mL). Return to meat and bring to a boil.

Mix flour in second amount of water until smooth. Stir into boiling meat until it boils again and thickens. Makes 4 servings.

NUTRITION GUIDE	1 serving contains:	
	Energy	183 Calories (766 kJ)
	Cholesterol	49 mg
	Sodium	268 mg
	Fat	6 g

SWISS STEAK

Tender meat with a bit of a nip to the gravy. Tiny new potatoes will make this a superb meal.

Round steak, cut in 4 pieces, all visible fat removed	**1 lb.**	**454 g**
Celery ribs, cut in 4 pieces each	**4**	**4**
Large onions, cut in 8 wedges each	**2**	**2**
Canned tomatoes	**14 oz.**	**398 mL**
Liquid sweetener	**¹/₄ tsp.**	**1 mL**
Worcestershire sauce	**1 tbsp.**	**15 mL**
Pepper	**¹/₄ tsp.**	**1 mL**
All-purpose flour	**4 tsp.**	**20 mL**
Water	**3 tbsp.**	**50 mL**

Brown steak under broiler. Place in 2 quart (2.5 L) casserole.

Add celery and onion.

Put tomatoes, liquid sweetener, Worcestershire sauce and pepper into medium saucepan. Heat until it boils.

Mix flour with water in cup until smooth. Stir into boiling tomatoes until it returns to a boil and thickens. Pour over casserole. Cover. Bake in 350°F (175°C) oven for about 2 hours until meat is fork tender. Makes 4 servings.

Pictured on page 71.

NUTRITION GUIDE	**1 serving contains:**	
	Energy	201 Calories (840 kJ)
	Cholesterol	49 mg
	Sodium	311 mg
	Fat	3 g

Paré Pointer

He has the best recipe for his speeches. They always include shortening.

Tender cubes of economical steak.

Vegetable cooking oil	1½ tbsp.	25 mL
Round steak, cubed, all visible fat removed	1 lb.	454 g
Water	½ cup	125 mL
Water to cover		
Large onion, chunked or sliced	1	1
Salt	¼ tsp.	1 mL
Pepper	¼ tsp.	1 mL
Thyme	¼ tsp.	1 mL

Heat cooking oil in frying pan. Add cubed meat. Sauté until meat is well browned on all sides. Transfer meat to saucepan.

Pour first amount of water into frying pan. Stir to loosen any brown bits in pan. Pour over meat. Add more water to cover. Bring to a boil. Cover and simmer for about 1½ hours until almost tender.

Add onion, salt, pepper and thyme. Continue to simmer about 20 minutes more, until onion is cooked and meat is very tender. Makes 4 servings.

NUTRITION GUIDE	**1 serving contains:**	
	Energy	195 Calories (816 kJ)
	Cholesterol	49 mg
	Sodium	234 mg
	Fat	8 g

If a horse has forelegs in front and two legs in back, does that add up to six legs?

TURKEY LOAF

A good way to utilize turkey. Bake a loaf.

Skim milk	1/4 cup	60 mL
Egg white (large)	1	1
Tomato sauce	7 1/2 oz.	213 mL
Dry bread crumbs	1/2 cup	125 mL
Pepper	1/4 tsp.	1 mL
Dry bread crumbs	1/2 cup	125 mL
Ground turkey (uncooked)	1 1/2 lbs.	670 g
Chopped onion	3/4 cup	175 mL
Grated carrot	2/3 cup	150 mL
All-purpose flour	2 tbsp.	30 mL
Parsley flakes	1 tsp.	5 mL

Place milk and egg white in large bowl. Beat with fork. Add tomato sauce, bread crumbs and pepper. Stir.

Add remaining ingredients. Mix well. Pack into 8 x 4 inch (20 x 10 cm) loaf pan which has been well coated with no-stick cooking spray. Bake in 350°F (175°C) oven for about 1 1/4 hours. Makes 6 servings.

NUTRITION GUIDE	1 serving contains:	
	Energy	275 Calories (1150 kJ)
	Cholesterol	82 mg
	Sodium	488 mg
	Fat	10 g

CHILI

There is nothing like a good bowl of chili. You may want to add more chili powder.

Lean ground beef	1 lb.	454 g
Chopped onion	1 cup	250 mL
Canned tomatoes, mashed	14 oz.	398 mL
Canned kidney beans	14 oz.	398 mL
Salt	1/4 tsp.	1 mL
Pepper	1/4 tsp.	1 mL
Chili powder	1 tsp.	5 mL
Granulated sugar	1 tsp.	5 mL

(continued on next page)

Spray large heavy saucepan with no-stick cooking spray. Scramble-fry ground beef and onion until no pink remains in meat and onion is soft.

Add remaining ingredients. Stir. Bring to a boil. Simmer, uncovered, for about 20 minutes. Makes 4²/₃ cups (1 L).

NUTRITION GUIDE	½ cup/125 mL contains:	
	Energy	190 Calories (793 kJ)
	Cholesterol	32 mg
	Sodium	392 mg
	Fat	9 g

BAKED BEEF DISH

Tender beef cubes with rich gravy.

Vegetable cooking oil	1 tbsp.	15 mL
Lean beef, cubed, all visible fat removed	1 lb.	454 g
All-purpose flour	3 tbsp.	50 mL
Parsley flakes	½ tsp.	2 mL
Pepper	¼ tsp.	1 mL
Salt	¼ tsp.	1 mL
Water	1½ cups	375 mL
Red wine (or alcohol-free wine)	1 tbsp.	15 mL
Chopped onion	1 cup	250 mL
Rolled oats	¼ cup	50 mL

Heat cooking oil in frying pan. Add cubed beef. Brown beef on all sides. Be sure to brown very well.

Sprinkle with flour, parsley, pepper and salt. Mix. Stir in water and wine until it boils and thickens. Transfer to 2 quart (2.5 L) casserole.

Add onion and rolled oats. Stir to distribute evenly. Cover. Cook in 300°F (150°C) oven about 2½ to 3 hours until meat is very tender. Makes 4 servings.

NUTRITION GUIDE	1 serving contains:	
	Energy	274 Calories (1146 kJ)
	Cholesterol	46 mg
	Sodium	242 mg
	Fat	12 g

PORK AND MOCK KRAUT

Lots of zip to this, but not too much. More chili powder can be added as desired.

Vegetable cooking oil	2 tbsp.	30 mL
Lean pork steak, cubed, all visible fat removed	1½ lbs.	680 g
Garlic clove, minced (or ¼ tsp., 1 mL, garlic powder)	1	1
Water	1½ cups	350 mL
Vinegar	3 tbsp.	50 mL
Chili powder	2 tsp.	10 mL
Beef bouillon packet (35% less salt)	1 x ¼ oz.	1 x 6.5 g
Oregano	1 tsp.	5 mL
Pepper	¼ tsp.	1 mL
Chopped or sliced onion	1½ cups	350 mL
Grated cabbage, packed	4 cups	900 mL
Grated, peeled cooking apple	1 cup	225 mL
Vinegar	1 tbsp.	15 mL

Heat cooking oil in large heavy saucepan. Add meat and garlic. Brown well.

Add next 6 ingredients. Stir. Bring to a boil. Cover and simmer about 1 hour until tender and no pink remains in meat.

Add remaining ingredients. Mix. Cook about 20 to 25 minutes until onion, cabbage and apple are soft. Makes 6 servings.

NUTRITION GUIDE	1 serving contains:	
	Energy	273 Calories (1142 kJ)
	Cholesterol	78 mg
	Sodium	183 mg
	Fat	10 g

A good colorful stir-fry. Fresh tomatoes give this a real lift.

Vegetable cooking oil	1 tsp.	5 mL
Thinly sliced celery	1 cup	250 mL
Green onions, sliced	2	2
Bok choy or cabbage, cut in large bite size pieces	3 cups	700 mL
Water	1/4 cup	60 mL
Vegetable cooking oil	1 tbsp.	15 mL
Lean pork steak, cut in thin strips, all visible fat removed	1 lb.	454 g
Cornstarch	2 tsp.	10 mL
Beef bouillon packet (35% less salt)	1 x 1/4 oz.	1 x 6.5 g
Water	1/2 cup	125 mL
Light soy sauce (40% less salt)	1 tbsp.	15 mL
Garlic powder	1/4 tsp.	1 mL
Ginger	1/4 tsp.	1 mL
Medium tomatoes, cut bite size	3	3
Fresh spinach or dark green lettuce, cut in strips, packed	1 cup	250 mL
Canned miniature corn cobs cut in 1/2 inch (1 cm) pieces	1/2 cup	125 mL

Heat first amount of cooking oil in wok or frying pan. Add celery, onion and bok choy. Stir-fry for about 1 minute.

Add first amount of water. Cover and cook slowly until tender, about 5 to 7 minutes. Remove to bowl.

Heat second amount of cooking oil in wok. Add thin meat strips. If meat is partially frozen it is easier to cut thinly. Stir-fry about 15 minutes until browned and no pink remains in meat.

In small bowl mix next 6 ingredients. Add to meat. Stir until it boils and thickens. Add cooked vegetables. Heat and stir.

Add tomatoes, spinach and corn. Cover. Allow to heat through for about 1 minute. Makes 4 servings.

Pictured on cover.

NUTRITION GUIDE	1 serving contains:	
	Energy	237 Calories (991 kJ)
	Cholesterol	64 mg
	Sodium	442 mg
	Fat	8 g

SESAME CHICKEN

Tasty and quick.

Vegetable cooking oil	2 tsp.	10 mL
Plain chicken fillets, 4 oz. (113 g) each	4	4
Apple juice, unsweetened	½ cup	125 mL
Chopped green onion	2 tbsp.	30 mL
Sesame seeds, toasted in 350°F (175°C) oven until browned	2 tsp.	10 mL

Add cooking oil to frying pan and heat. Brown fillets on both sides until cooked and quite brown, about 5 minutes.

Add apple juice and onion. Simmer until approximately ½ the juice is boiled away.

Serve individually or on platter. Spoon remaining juice over top. Sprinkle with sesame seeds. Makes 4 servings.

Pictured on cover.

NUTRITION GUIDE	1 serving contains:	
	Energy	170 Calories (712 kJ)
	Cholesterol	66 mg
	Sodium	75 mg
	Fat	5 g

1. Chicken Casserole page 99
2. Chicken Pie Casserole page 92
3. Carrot Magic page 139
4. Lemon Turkey page 95
5. Peas With Mushrooms page 138

Large enough for a party. May be halved for family use. Chicken and dressing in one casserole. If on a sodium restricted diet, use low sodium canned soup in ingredients.

Chicken breasts, halved, skin removed	6	6
Boiling water		
Low-fat plain yogurt (less than 1% MF)	1½ cups	350 mL
Condensed cream of mushroom soup	10 oz.	284 mL
All-purpose flour	3 tbsp.	50 mL
Sliced, fresh mushrooms	2 cups	450 mL
Dry bread crumbs	1½ cups	350 mL
Onion flakes	1 tbsp.	15 mL
Poultry seasoning	½ tsp.	2 mL
Parsley flakes	½ tsp.	2 mL
Celery flakes	½ tsp.	2 mL
Pepper	¹/₁₆ tsp.	0.5 mL
Chicken bouillon packet (35% less salt)	1 × ¼ oz.	1 × 6.5 g
Boiling water	6 tbsp.	100 mL

Cook chicken breasts in boiling water to cover in covered saucepan until tender. Cool to handle. Remove bones. Cut meat into cubes.

Stir yogurt, soup and flour in medium bowl until flour is well mixed. Add mushrooms and chicken. Stir. Turn into 3 quart (4 L) casserole.

Measure next 6 ingredients into bowl. Mix.

Dissolve bouillon powder in boiling water. Add to crumb mixture. Stir. Spread over chicken. Cover. Cook in 350°F (175°C) oven for about 35 to 40 minutes until bubbling hot. Makes 12 servings.

NUTRITION GUIDE	**1 serving contains:**	
	Energy	245 Calories (1024 kJ)
	Cholesterol	74 mg
	Sodium	509 mg
	Fat	6 g

CHICKEN PIE CASSEROLE

A tender biscuit crust tops this easy-to-make dish. Serve with a salad for a complete meal. If on a sodium restricted diet, use low sodium canned soup in ingredients.

Margarine	2 tsp.	10 mL
Chopped onion	1/2 cup	125 mL
Condensed cream of mushroom soup	10 oz.	284 mL
Skim milk	1/2 cup	125 mL
Chopped, cooked chicken	1 1/4 cups	275 mL
Cubed, cooked potato	1 cup	225 mL
Sliced, cooked carrot	1 cup	225 mL
Thyme	1/8 tsp.	0.5 mL
TOPPING		
All-purpose flour	1 cup	225 mL
Baking powder	2 tsp.	10 mL
Salt	1/4 tsp.	1 mL
Margarine	2 tbsp.	30 mL
Skim milk	6 tbsp.	100 mL

Heat margarine in frying pan. Add onion. Sauté until soft but not brown.

Stir in next 6 ingredients. Keep hot.

Topping: Combine flour, baking powder and salt in bowl. Cut in margarine until crumbly.

Add milk. Stir to form a soft ball. If too dry, add a bit more milk. Turn chicken mixture into 2 quart (2.5 L) casserole. Roll dough on lightly floured surface slightly larger than casserole. Place over top pressing against edge all around. Prick through top in several places with fork. Bake in 425°F (220°C) oven about 20 minutes until hot and top is raised and browned. Serves 4.

Pictured on page 89.

NUTRITION GUIDE	**1 serving contains:**	
	Energy	460 Calories (1926 kJ)
	Cholesterol	43 mg
	Sodium	975 mg
	Fat	17 g

An unusual combination of chicken, pineapple, raisins and spices. Be different.

Chicken legs (drumstick and thigh connected)	4	4
Vegetable cooking oil	1 tsp.	5 mL
Chopped onion	1/3 cup	75 mL
Crushed pineapple, unsweetened, with juice	1 cup	225 mL
Raisins or currants	1/4 cup	50 mL
Prepared orange juice, unsweetened	1/3 cup	75 mL
Pepper	1/4 tsp.	1 mL
Cinnamon	1/8 tsp.	0.5 mL
Garlic powder	1/4 tsp.	1 mL

Remove skin from chicken. Pat dry with paper towel. Brush with cooking oil. Brown under broiler. Place in small roaster.

Stir remaining 7 ingredients together in bowl. Pour over chicken. Cover. Cook in 350°F (175°C) oven for about 1 to 1½ hours until tender. Makes 4 servings.

NUTRITION GUIDE	1 serving contains:	
	Energy	251 Calories (1049 kJ)
	Cholesterol	104 mg
	Sodium	115 mg
	Fat	6 g

When he stood up to be counted, someone took his seat.

CHEESY CHICKEN

This looks so appealing. Flattened chicken breasts covered with cheese. Just the right amount of spice.

Chicken breasts, halved, skin and bone removed	2	2
Vegetable cooking oil	2 tsp.	10 mL
Part-skim ricotta cheese, crumbled (less than 2% MF)	1/2 cup	125 mL
Chives	1/2 tsp.	2 mL
Parsley flakes	1/4 tsp.	1 mL
Thyme	1/16 tsp.	0.5 mL
Pepper	1/8 tsp.	0.5 mL
Process skim mozzarella cheese slices (7% MF)	4	4

Flatten chicken breast to make same thickness. Blot dry with paper towel. Brush with cooking oil. Broil under medium heat about 2 minutes each side.

In small bowl mash ricotta cheese with fork. Add chives, parsley, thyme and pepper. Divide over chicken.

Lay cheese slices over top. Broil until browned and heated through. Makes 4 servings.

NUTRITION GUIDE	1 serving contains:	
	Energy	237 Calories (993 kJ)
	Cholesterol	78 mg
	Sodium	117 mg
	Fat	8 g

QUITE THE CHICK

Just spread sauce over the chicken and bake. Quite the dish.

Chicken parts, skin removed	3 lbs.	1.36 kg
Ketchup	1/3 cup	75 mL
Beef bouillon packets (35% less salt)	2 x 1/4 oz.	2 x 6.5 g
Onion flakes	1 tbsp.	15 mL
Light soy sauce (40% less salt)	2 tsp.	10 mL
Prepared mustard	1 tsp.	5 mL
Water	3 tbsp.	50 mL

(continued on next page)

Arrange chicken parts in 3 quart (4 L) casserole.

Mix next 6 ingredients in small bowl. Spoon over chicken being sure to get some on every piece. Cover. Cook in 350°F (175°C) for 1 to 1½ hours until tender. Makes 6 servings.

NUTRITION GUIDE	1 serving contains:	
	Energy	155 Calories (650 kJ)
	Cholesterol	76 mg
	Sodium	548 mg
	Fat	4 g

LEMON TURKEY

Turkey cutlets glisten beneath a transparent sauce.

Plain turkey cutlets	**1½ lbs.**	**680 g**
Vegetable cooking oil	**1½ tsp.**	**7 mL**
LEMON SAUCE		
Lemon juice	**¼ cup**	**60 mL**
Water	**1 cup**	**225 mL**
Parsley flakes	**½ tsp.**	**2 mL**
Cornstarch	**2 tbsp.**	**30 mL**
Paprika, sprinkle		
Liquid sweetener	**1 tsp.**	**5 mL**

Brush turkey with cooking oil. Broil 2 to 3 minutes on each side until cooked.

Lemon Sauce: Combine first 4 ingredients in small saucepan. Mix well. Heat and stir until it boils and thickens. Makes 1 cup (225 mL).

Sprinkle cutlets with paprika. Add sweetener to sauce. Spoon over cutlets. Makes 6 servings.

Pictured on page 89.

NUTRITION GUIDE	1 serving contains:	
	Energy	149 Calories (621 kJ)
	Cholesterol	83 mg
	Sodium	70 mg
	Fat	3 g

Lemon Chicken: Use chicken cutlets instead of turkey.

DILLED CHICKEN

Good dill flavored sauce enhances this dish. Makes a pleasant change.

Chicken parts, skin removed	3 lbs.	1.36 kg
All-purpose flour	$\frac{1}{3}$ cup	75 mL
Chicken bouillon packets	2 x $\frac{1}{4}$ oz.	2 x 6.5 g
(35% less salt)		
Dill weed	1 tsp.	5 mL
Paprika	$\frac{1}{4}$ tsp.	1 mL
Pepper	$\frac{1}{4}$ tsp.	1 mL
Skim milk	1$\frac{1}{4}$ cups	275 mL
Low-fat plain yogurt (less than 1% MF)	1 cup	225 mL

Paprika, good sprinkle

Arrange chicken pieces in 3 quart (4 L) casserole.

Mix flour, bouillon powder, dill weed, first amount of paprika, and pepper in saucepan. Stir in about $\frac{1}{2}$ of the milk until smooth. Stir in remaining milk and yogurt. Heat and stir until it boils and thickens. Pour over chicken.

Sprinkle with paprika. Cook, uncovered, in 350°F (175°C) oven for about 1$\frac{1}{2}$ hours until tender. Makes 6 servings.

NUTRITION GUIDE	1 serving contains:	
	Energy	202 Calories (845 kJ)
	Cholesterol	78 mg
	Sodium	336 mg
	Fat	4 g

Paré Pointer

The health clinic kept bandages in the refrigerator so they could use them for cold cuts.

Makes a splendid lunch.

Skim milk	**1¹/₂ cups**	**350 mL**
All-purpose flour	**¹/₄ cup**	**60 mL**
Skim milk	**¹/₂ cup**	**125 mL**
Sliced, fresh mushrooms	**2 cups**	**450 mL**
Water	**¹/₂ cup**	**125 mL**
Chicken bouillon packets (35% less salt)	**2 × ¹/₄ oz.**	**2 × 6.5 g**
Pepper	**¹/₈ tsp.**	**0.5 mL**
Finely chopped red pepper	**¹/₃ cup**	**75 mL**
Diced, cooked chicken	**1¹/₂ cups**	**350 mL**
Whole wheat bread slices, toasted, unbuttered	**8**	**8**

Heat first amount of milk in heavy saucepan until it boils.

Meanwhile, mix flour in second amount of milk in small bowl until smooth. Stir into boiling milk until it returns to a boil and thickens.

Cook mushrooms in water in another saucepan about 10 minutes until tender. Drain. Add to sauce.

Add next 4 ingredients. Stir. Heat through.

Serve on slices of toast. Serves 4.

NUTRITION GUIDE	1 serving contains:	
	Energy	337 Calories (1409 kJ)
	Cholesterol	54 mg
	Sodium	709 mg
	Fat	6 g

Paré Pointer

A quick quack is a fast duck.

CHICKEN FILLETS IN CREAM

A mild mustard sauce covers chicken before baking. Yogurt gives the creamy texture.

Plain chicken or turkey fillets, **4 oz. (113 g) each**	6	6
Chicken bouillon packet (35% less salt)	1 × ¼ oz.	1 × 6.5 g
Hot water	¼ cup	60 mL
Grated Parmesan cheese	3 tbsp.	50 mL
Prepared mustard	1 tbsp.	15 mL
Thyme	¼ tsp.	1 mL
Low-fat plain yogurt (less than 1% MF)	1 cup	225 mL
All-purpose flour	2 tbsp.	30 mL

Arrange 3 fillets in 2 quart (2.5 L) casserole.

Dissolve bouillon powder in hot water in cup. Add cheese, mustard and thyme. Stir.

Mix yogurt and flour in small bowl. Add cheese mixture. Stir. Spoon ½ mixture over fillets in casserole. Lay second 3 fillets over top. Spoon rest of sauce over all being sure all fillets are covered. Bake, uncovered, in 350°F (175°C) oven for about 1 hour until meat is tender. Makes 6 servings.

NUTRITION GUIDE	1 serving contains:	
	Energy	130 Calories (545 kJ)
	Cholesterol	47 mg
	Sodium	257 mg
	Fat	2 g

Paré Pointer

How come we water a horse but milk a cow?

Dark red in color and a hint of sweetness. Lots of sauce to spoon over rice or potatoes.

Chicken thighs, skin removed	3 lbs.	1.36 kg
Liquid gravy browner	2 tsp.	10 mL
Medium onion, cut in short strips	1	1
Thinly sliced celery	½ cup	125 mL
Finely chopped green pepper	¼ cup	50 mL
Tomato paste	½ x 5½ oz.	½ x 156 mL
Water	1 cup	225 mL
Vinegar	⅓ cup	75 mL
Worcestershire sauce	1 tbsp.	15 mL
Liquid sweetener	2 tsp.	10 mL
Pepper	¼ tsp.	1 mL
Onion powder	⅛ tsp.	0.5 mL
Cinnamon	⅛ tsp.	0.5 mL

There are about 12 thighs in 3 lb. (1.36 kg) package of chicken. Brush chicken thighs with gravy browner. Let stand 30 minutes. Arrange in 3 quart (4 L) casserole.

Sprinkle with onion, celery and green pepper.

Mix remaining 8 ingredients in bowl. Pour over all. Cover. Bake in 350°F (175°C) oven for about 1½ hours until chicken is tender. Makes 6 servings.

Pictured on page 89.

NUTRITION GUIDE	1 serving contains:	
	Energy	186 Calories (778 kJ)
	Cholesterol	107 mg
	Sodium	257 mg
	Fat	5 g

Paré Pointer

To cure a pig's sore skin use oinkment.

CHICKEN AND RICE BAKE

A meal in a dish. No pre-cooking is required. If on a sodium restricted diet, use low sodium canned soup in ingredients.

Condensed cream of chicken soup	10 oz.	284 mL
Skim milk	1/2 cup	125 mL
Beef bouillon packets (35% less salt)	2 x 1/4 oz.	2 x 6.5 g
Onion flakes	1 1/2 tsp.	7 mL
Parsley flakes	1/2 tsp.	2 mL
Onion powder	1/4 tsp.	1 mL
Minute rice	3/4 cup	175 mL
Whole chicken breasts, halved, skin removed	2	2

Mix first 6 ingredients in bowl. Set aside.

Place rice in 8 inch (20 cm) casserole. Arrange 4 chicken breast halves over rice. Spoon soup mixture over chicken. Cover. Bake in 350°F (175°C) oven for about 1 1/2 to 2 hours until chicken is very tender. Makes 4 servings.

NUTRITION GUIDE	1 serving contains:	
	Energy	234 Calories (977 kJ)
	Cholesterol	43 mg
	Sodium	654 mg
	Fat	6 g

CHICKEN SOY BOIL

Cook the chicken right in the marinade. Cook and marinate at the same time. Not for salt restricted diets.

Water	1/2 cup	125 mL
Light soy sauce (40% less salt)	1/4 cup	60 mL
Ginger	1/4 tsp.	1 mL
Liquid sweetener	2 1/4 tsp.	11 mL
Chicken parts, skin removed	3 lbs.	1.36 kg

(continued on next page)

Measure first 4 ingredients into large saucepan. Stir well.

Arrange chicken parts in saucepan. Bring to a boil. Simmer, covered, for about 35 to 45 minutes until tender. Turn chicken occasionally as it cooks. Add a bit of water if needed. Makes 6 servings.

NUTRITION GUIDE	1 serving contains:	
	Energy	138 Calories (577 kJ)
	Cholesterol	76 mg
	Sodium	522 mg
	Fat	3 g

FISH CREOLE

Cooked on top of the stove, this is red-topped due to the addition of tomato paste. Onion adds flavor.

Halibut fish steaks (or other), 4 oz. (113 g) each	**1¹/₂ lbs.**	**680 g**
Pepper, sprinkle		
Finely chopped onion	**¹/₂ cup**	**125 mL**
Tomato paste	**¹/₂ × 5¹/₂ oz.**	**¹/₂ × 156 mL**
Water	**¹/₄ cup**	**60 mL**
Liquid sweetener	**¹/₈ tsp.**	**0.5 mL**
Garlic powder	**¹/₄ tsp.**	**1 mL**

Place fish steaks in frying pan in single layer. Sprinkle with pepper and onion.

Stir tomato paste, water, sweetener and garlic powder together. Pour over fish. Bring to a slow simmer. Cover and simmer for about 20 minutes. Add a bit of water if needed if it gets too thick and dry. Makes 6 servings.

Pictured on page 107.

NUTRITION GUIDE	1 serving contains:	
	Energy	142 Calories (596 kJ)
	Cholesterol	36 mg
	Sodium	71 mg
	Fat	3 g

BROILED COD

Topped with asparagus and a cheese sauce.

Cod fillets	1½ lbs.	680 g
Lemon juice	1 tbsp.	15 mL
Salt, sprinkle		
Pepper, sprinkle		
Skim milk	¾ cup	175 mL
All-purpose flour	2 tbsp.	30 mL
Grated low-fat sharp Cheddar cheese (less than 21% MF)	¾ cup	175 mL
Frozen asparagus spears, cooked	10 oz.	284 g

Line baking tray with foil. Spray foil with no-stick cooking spray. Arrange cod fillets on foil. Drizzle with lemon juice. Sprinkle with salt and pepper. Broil 6 inches (15 cm) from heat for about 10 minutes.

Meanwhile, mix part of the milk with flour in small saucepan until smooth. Add rest of milk. Heat and stir until it boils and thickens.

Remove from heat. Stir in cheese until it melts.

Place asparagus spears over fish. Spoon sauce over top. Broil again for about 3 minutes until cheese sauce begins to brown. Makes 6 servings.

Pictured on page 107.

NUTRITION GUIDE	1 serving contains:	
	Energy	162 Calories (679 kJ)
	Cholesterol	58 mg
	Sodium	486 mg
	Fat	4 g

Paré Pointer

Combine Dracula with a knight from long ago and you have a bite in shining armor.

Fish fillets are sandwiched with stuffing. Contains chopped tomatoes.

Sole fillets	1 lb.	454 g
Dry bread crumbs	³/₄ cup	175 mL
Medium tomatoes, peeled and chopped	2	2
Pepper, sprinkle		
Water	2 tbsp.	30 mL
Onion flakes	1 tsp.	5 mL
Basil	¹/₂ tsp.	2 mL
Poultry seasoning	¹/₄ tsp.	1 mL
Lemon wedges	4	4

Spray pan, large enough to hold half the fillets in single layer, with no-stick cooking spray. Lay half the sole fillets in pan.

Combine next 7 ingredients in bowl. Mix. Spread over fillets. Lay remaining fillets over top. Cover. Bake in 350°F (175°C) oven about 40 to 50 minutes until fish flakes when tested with fork.

Serve with lemon wedges. Makes 4 servings.

N U T R I T I O N G U I D E	1 serving contains:	
	Energy	206 Calories (860 kJ)
	Cholesterol	55 mg
	Sodium	257 mg
	Fat	3 g

Paré Pointer

That photographer is suspect. First he shot people and then he blew them up.

SALMON LOAF

A scrumptious loaf. Very tender.

Skim milk	³/₄ cup	175 mL
All-purpose flour	1 tbsp.	15 mL
Salt	¹/₄ tsp.	1 mL
Pepper	¹/₄ tsp.	1 mL
Paprika	¹/₄ tsp.	1 mL
Lemon juice	2 tbsp.	30 mL
Cracker crumbs	¹/₂ cup	125 mL
Canned salmon, drained, skin and round bones removed	2 × 7¹/₂ oz.	2 × 213 g
Egg whites (large), room temperature	2	2

Mix skim milk and flour in medium saucepan until no lumps remain. Add salt, pepper and paprika. Stir over medium heat until it boils. Remove from heat.

Stir in lemon juice, cracker crumbs and salmon. Round salmon bones may be used if crushed.

Beat egg whites in small bowl until stiff. Fold into salmon mixture. Pack into 8 × 4 inch (20 × 10 cm) loaf pan which has been coated with no-stick cooking spray. Bake in 350°F (175°C) oven for about 1¹/₂ hours. Cut into 6 slices.

NUTRITION GUIDE	1 slice contains:	
	Energy	154 Calories (647 kJ)
	Cholesterol	18 mg
	Sodium	481 mg
	Fat	8 g

Paré Pointer

The police locked up the rock star when they heard he had a record.

A good way to serve tuna.

Water	1/4 cup	60 mL
Egg white (large)	1	1
All-purpose flour	2 tbsp.	30 mL
Evaporated skim milk	13 1/2 oz.	385 mL
Canned pimiento (or green pepper), chopped	1 tbsp.	15 mL
Parsley flakes	1 tsp.	5 mL
Prepared mustard	1/2 tsp.	2 mL
Worcestershire sauce	1/2 tsp.	2 mL
Canned white tuna, water packed, drained, broken up	2 x 6 1/2 oz.	2 x 184 g
Margarine	2 tbsp.	30 mL
Dry bread crumbs	1/2 cup	125 mL

In small mixing bowl beat water, egg white and flour until smooth. Add milk, pimiento, parsley, mustard and Worcestershire sauce.

Place tuna in 2 quart (2.5 L) casserole. Pour milk sauce over top. Lift tuna here and there to allow sauce to penetrate and mix.

Melt margarine in small saucepan. Stir in bread crumbs. Sprinkle over casserole. Bake, uncovered, in 350°F (175°C) oven for about 35 minutes until bubbly hot. Makes 2 1/8 cups (480 mL).

NUTRITION GUIDE	1/2 cup/125 mL contains:	
	Energy	299 Calories (1253 kJ)
	Cholesterol	34 mg
	Sodium	597 mg
	Fat	8 g

Paré Pointer

When he wanted to learn how to fight all he did was study scrapbooks.

FRIED COD

The easiest way to cook fish for people who want theirs fried. Very little fat is needed in a teflon pan.

Cod fillets	**1¹/₂ lbs.**	**680 g**
Fine dry bread crumbs	**¹/₃ cup**	**75 mL**
Margarine	**1 tbsp.**	**15 mL**
Pepper, sprinkle		
Lemon juice	**1 tbsp.**	**15 mL**

Coat fish fillets with bread crumbs.

Melt margarine in teflon-coated frying pan large enough to hold all fillets in single layer. Arrange fillets in frying pan. Cook until brown. Turn to brown other side. Fish should flake when tested with fork.

Sprinkle with pepper and lemon juice. Makes 6 servings.

NUTRITION GUIDE	**1 serving contains:**	
	Energy	135 Calories (566 kJ)
	Cholesterol	49 mg
	Sodium	130 mg
	Fat	3 g

1. Blackened Snapper page 110
2. Fish Creole page 101
3. Broiled Cod page 102
4. Oven Baked Fries page 146
5. Coleslaw page 117

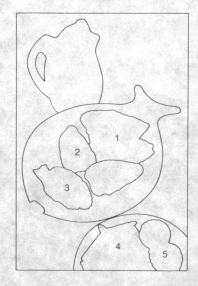

The crunchy topping finishes off the cream-sauced fish.

Fish fillets (cod, sole, or your choice)	**1¹/₂ lbs.**	**680 g**
Skim milk	**1 cup**	**225 mL**
All-purpose flour	**2 tbsp.**	**30 mL**
Skim milk	**¹/₄ cup**	**60 mL**
Salt	**¹/₄ tsp.**	**1 mL**
Pepper, sprinkle		
Parsley flakes	**¹/₂ tsp.**	**2 mL**
TOPPING		
Margarine	**2 tbsp.**	**30 mL**
Dry bread crumbs	**¹/₂ cup**	**125 mL**
Water	**2 tbsp.**	**30 mL**
Grated low-fat sharp Cheddar cheese (less than 21% MF)	**¹/₄ cup**	**60 mL**

Lay fish fillets in bottom of 3 quart (4 L) casserole.

Heat first amount of skim milk in saucepan until it boils.

Meanwhile mix flour with remaining milk until smooth. Mix in salt, pepper and parsley. Stir into boiling milk until it returns to a boil and thickens. Pour over fish. Lift each fillet gently with a fork to allow a bit of sauce to run underneath.

Topping: Melt margarine in small saucepan. Stir in bread crumbs, water and cheese. Sprinkle over casserole. Bake, uncovered, in 350°F (175°C) oven 40 to 50 minutes. Makes 6 servings.

NUTRITION GUIDE	**1 serving contains:**	
	Energy	207 Calories (866 kJ)
	Cholesterol	53 mg
	Sodium	398 mg
	Fat	6 g

BLACKENED SNAPPER

It's hot all right! And it's so good. Cut the amount of cayenne pepper if you must.

CAJUN SEASONING

Garlic powder	**1 tsp.**	**5 mL**
Onion powder	**1 tsp.**	**5 mL**
Chili powder	**1 tsp.**	**5 mL**
Paprika	**1 tsp.**	**5 mL**
Pepper	**¹/₂ tsp.**	**2 mL**
Cayenne pepper	**¹/₂ tsp.**	**2 mL**
Thyme	**¹/₄ tsp.**	**1 mL**
Red snapper fillets	**1¹/₂ lbs.**	**680 g**
Vegetable cooking oil	**1¹/₂ tbsp.**	**25 mL**

Cajun Seasoning: Measure first 7 ingredients into shallow soup bowl. Stir well to mix.

Heat heavy frying pan until very hot. A cast iron pan is best. Pat fillets dry with paper towel. Coat fillets with cooking oil then with seasoning. Place in hot frying pan that has been sprayed with no-stick cooking spray. Cook 2 to 3 minutes. Turn and cook 2 to 3 minutes more. Makes 6 servings.

Pictured on page 107.

NUTRITION GUIDE	1 serving contains:	
	Energy	151 Calories (631 kJ)
	Cholesterol	42 mg
	Sodium	78 mg
	Fat	5 g

BAKED SOLE

A dark spicy covering gives just a hint of bread stuffing.

Sole fillets (or other)	**1 lb.**	**454 g**
Lemon juice	**1 tbsp.**	**15 mL**
Powdered rosemary	**³/₄ tsp.**	**4 mL**
Pepper	**¹/₄ tsp.**	**1 mL**
Lemon wedges	**4**	**4**

(continued on next page)

Arrange sole fillets in baking pan which has been sprayed with no-stick cooking spray. Drizzle lemon juice over top. Mix rosemary and pepper. Sprinkle over fillets. Bake, uncovered, in 350°F (175°C) oven for about 20 minutes until fish flakes when tested with fork.

Serve with lemon wedges. Makes 4 servings.

NUTRITION GUIDE	1 serving contains:	
	Energy	108 Calories (450 kJ)
	Cholesterol	55 mg
	Sodium	92 mg
	Fat	2 g

LUNCH TIME CASSEROLE

Easy to make, not heavy but wholesome. Cabbage, ham, apple and onion make a good combination.

Grated cabbage	**4 cups**	**900 mL**
Canned ham flakes (33% less salt),	**2 × 6.5 oz.**	**2 × 184 g**
broken up		
Chopped, peeled apple	**1 cup**	**225 mL**
Chopped onion	**1/2 cup**	**125 mL**
Parsley flakes	**1 tsp.**	**5 mL**
Skim milk	**1/2 cup**	**125 mL**

In large bowl combine cabbage, ham, apple, onion and parsley. Stir to distribute ingredients. Turn into 2 quart (2.5 L) casserole.

Pour milk over top. Cover. Bake in 350°F (175°C) oven for about 45 minutes until vegetables are cooked. Makes 4 servings.

NUTRITION GUIDE	1 serving contains:	
	Energy	287 Calories (1202 kJ)
	Cholesterol	46 mg
	Sodium	872 mg
	Fat	18 g

PORK APPLE STEAKS

Pork steaks are browned, spread with spicy applesauce and baked.

Pork steak, all visible fat removed	2 lbs.	900 g
Canned applesauce, unsweetened	14 oz.	398 mL
Cinnamon	1/4 tsp.	1 mL
Nutmeg	1/4 tsp.	1 mL
Salt	1/4 tsp.	1 mL
Pepper	1/4 tsp.	1 mL
Sherry (or non-alcohol sherry)	1/4 cup	50 mL

Brown steak on both sides in frying pan sprayed with no-stick cooking spray or under broiler. Arrange in baking pan large enough to hold in single layer.

Combine remaining ingredients in small bowl. Stir. Spoon about 1/2 over steak. Cook, uncovered, in 350°F (175°C) oven for about 20 minutes. Turn steaks over. Spoon second 1/2 sauce over. Return to oven to cook for about 30 minutes more until tender. Makes 8 servings.

NUTRITION GUIDE	1 serving contains:	
	Energy	154 Calories (645 kJ)
	Cholesterol	64 mg
	Sodium	142 mg
	Fat	3 g

HAM STEAK SURPRISE

The surprise is the turkey. This has the flavor of clove-studded ham. Sauce is plentiful.

Plain turkey cutlets	1 lb.	454 g
Dry mustard powder	1/2 tsp.	2 mL
SPICED SAUCE		
Apple juice, unsweetened	1 cup	225 mL
Cinnamon	1/4 tsp.	1 mL
Cloves	1/8 tsp.	0.5 mL
Lemon juice	1 tsp.	5 mL
Liquid sweetener	1/2 tsp.	2 mL
Cornstarch	1 tbsp.	15 mL
Water	1 tbsp.	15 mL

(continued on next page)

Sprinkle turkey with mustard. Rub in. Arrange in cake pan large enough to hold in single layer. Bake, uncovered, in 350°F (175°C) oven for 30 minutes.

Spiced Sauce: Heat first 5 ingredients in small saucepan until it boils.

Mix cornstarch and water in small cup. Stir into boiling liquid until it returns to a boil and thickens. Spoon over turkey. Makes 4 servings.

NUTRITION GUIDE	1 serving contains:	
	Energy	177 Calories (740 kJ)
	Cholesterol	74 mg
	Sodium	82 mg
	Fat	4 g

CAULIFLOWER SALAD

Very different. Red radish and green onion brighten the cauliflower. Very good.

Thinly sliced cauliflower pieces	**2 cups**	**450 mL**
Radishes, cut in short sticks	**4**	**4**
Chopped green onion	**1 tbsp.**	**15 mL**
DRESSING		
Light salad dressing (or mayonnaise)	**6 tbsp.**	**100 mL**
Skim milk	**4 tsp.**	**20 mL**
Garlic powder, just a pinch (optional)		

Toss first 3 ingredients together in bowl.

Dressing: Mix all ingredients and pour over salad. Toss. Makes 2 cups (450 mL). Serves 4.

NUTRITION GUIDE	¹/₂ cup/125 mL contains:	
	Energy	81 Calories (335 kJ)
	Cholesterol	trace
	Sodium	186 mg
	Fat	6 g

CAESAR SALAD

Make this salad complete with dressing minus the egg. Serve grated Parmesan cheese on the side if desired.

CAESAR DRESSING

Low-fat cottage cheese (less than 1% MF)	$1/2$ cup	125 mL
Skim milk	$1/4$ cup	60 mL
Lemon juice	1 tbsp.	15 mL
Anchovy paste	1 tsp.	5 mL
Worcestershire sauce	$1/2$ tsp.	2 mL
Garlic clove	$1/2$	$1/2$
Pepper, sprinkle		
Grated Parmesan cheese	2 tbsp.	30 mL

SALAD

Head of Romaine lettuce	1	1
Croutons	$1^1/2$ cups	350 mL
Freshly grated pepper, generous sprinkle		

Caesar Dressing: Combine first 7 ingredients in blender. Process until smooth. Scrape into small container.

Stir in Parmesan cheese. Makes $2/3$ cup (150 mL).

Salad: Tear or cut lettuce into large bowl. Add croutons. Just before serving add dressing. Toss.

Grate pepper over top. Serves 6.

NUTRITION GUIDE

1 serving contains:

Energy	80 Calories (333 kJ)
Cholesterol	3 mg
Sodium	231 mg
Fat	1 g

Paré Pointer

A whooping crane is really a stork with pneumonia.

SPINACH AND MUSHROOM SALAD

You can also use your favorite greens in this salad. A very flavorful dressing.

FEISTY DRESSING

Low-fat cottage cheese (less than 1% MF)	1/2 cup	125 mL
Vinegar	4 tsp.	20 mL
Dill weed	1/8 tsp.	0.5 mL
Liquid sweetener	1/8 tsp.	0.5 mL

SALAD

Torn spinach or other greens, lightly packed	5 1/2 cups	1.24 L
Hard-boiled eggs, whites only, chopped	2	2
Sliced, fresh mushrooms	1 cup	225 mL
Croutons	1/2 cup	125 mL
Grated Parmesan cheese	2 tbsp.	30 mL

Feisty Dressing: Smooth first 4 ingredients in blender.

Salad: Tear spinach into large bowl. Add egg whites, mushrooms, croutons and cheese. Spoon dressing over salad. Toss. Makes 6 servings.

Pictured on page 143.

NUTRITION GUIDE	**1 serving contains:**	
	Energy	57 Calories (238 kJ)
	Cholesterol	2 mg
	Sodium	201 mg
	Fat	1 g

GREENS AND FRUIT SALAD

Contains orange segments, raisins and nuts.

Head of Romaine lettuce, or other greens	1	1
Mandarin orange segments, drained	10 oz.	184 mL
CREAMY DRESSING		
Low-fat cottage cheese, (less than 1% MF)	1/2 cup	125 mL
Skim milk	2 tbsp.	30 mL
Vinegar	1 1/2 tbsp.	25 mL
Liquid sweetener	1/2 tsp.	2 mL
Raisins	1/2 cup	125 mL
Chopped walnuts	1/4 cup	50 mL

Tear lettuce into large bowl. Add orange segments.

Creamy Dressing: Run cottage cheese, milk, vinegar and sweetener through blender to smooth. Pour into small bowl.

Stir in raisins and walnuts. Pour over lettuce and orange segments. Toss. Makes 6 servings.

Pictured on cover.

NUTRITION GUIDE	1serving contains:	
	Energy	113 Calories (472 kJ)
	Cholesterol	1 mg
	Sodium	94 mg
	Fat	4 g

FRENCH DRESSING

A pale paprika color. Tart enough for your favorite greens.

All-purpose flour	3 tbsp.	45 mL
Water	1 cup	250 mL
Vinegar	1/3 cup	75 mL
Salt	1/2 tsp.	2 mL
Dry mustard	1/2 tsp.	2 mL
Paprika	1/2 tsp.	2 mL
Onion powder	1/16 tsp.	0.5 mL
Garlic powder	1/16 tsp.	0.5 mL
Liquid sweetener	1 1/4 tsp.	6 mL

(continued on next page)

Mix flour with half of the water in small saucepan until smooth. Add remaining water. Add remaining ingredients. Heat and stir over medium heat until it boils and thickens. Remove from heat. Makes 1¹/₂ cups (350 mL).

NUTRITION GUIDE	1 tbsp./15 mL contains:	
	Energy	5 Calories (19 kJ)
	Cholesterol	0 mg
	Sodium	57 mg
	Fat	trace

COLESLAW

Dressing is very light with a hint of orange.

Grated cabbage	2 cups	450 mL
Grated carrot	¹/₄ cup	50 mL
Thinly sliced celery	¹/₂ cup	125 mL

COLESLAW DRESSING		
Low-fat plain yogurt (less than 1% MF)	6 tbsp.	90 mL
Frozen concentrated orange juice, unsweetened	2 tsp.	10 mL
Onion powder	¹/₄ tsp.	1 mL
Liquid sweetener	¹/₄ tsp.	1 mL

Freshly ground pepper

Combine cabbage, carrot and celery in bowl. Toss to mix.

Coleslaw Dressing: Mix next 4 ingredients in small bowl. Pour over cabbage mixture. Toss well. Turn into shallow serving bowl.

Sprinkle generously with freshly ground pepper. Makes 2 cups (450 mL).

Pictured on page 107.

NUTRITION GUIDE	¹/₂ cup/125 mL contains:	
	Energy	32 Calories (132 kJ)
	Cholesterol	trace
	Sodium	40 mg
	Fat	trace

CREAMY LIME SALAD

This is so rich tasting you would never guess that it doesn't contain regular cream cheese and real whipped cream.

Low calorie lime flavored gelatin (jelly powder), 4 serving size	1	1
Boiling water (use drained pineapple juice as part)	³/₄ cup	175 mL
Low-fat cream cheese, (less than 20% MF), softened	¹/₂ cup	125 mL
Cold water	³/₄ cup	175 mL
Crushed pineapple, unsweetened, drained	14 oz.	398 mL
Frozen whipped topping, thawed	1 cup	225 mL

Dissolve gelatin in boiling water in saucepan. Cool but don't thicken.

Beat cream cheese and water together in small mixing bowl until smooth. Add gelatin mixture. Beat slowly until mixed.

Stir in pineapple. Chill until syrupy.

Fold in whipped topping. Pour into 4 cup (900 mL) mold. Makes 3²/₃ cups (825 mL).

NUTRITION GUIDE	¹/₃ **cup/75 mL contains:**	
	Energy	62 Calories (261 kJ)
	Cholesterol	7 mg
	Sodium	81 mg
	Fat	3 g

TOMATO SALAD

A colorful addition to any meal. Excellent flavor in a mold.

Canned stewed tomatoes	14 oz.	398 mL
Low calorie lemon flavored gelatin (jelly powder), 4 serving size	1	1
Worcestershire sauce	¹/₂ tsp.	2 mL
Finely chopped apple	¹/₃ cup	75 mL
Finely chopped celery	¹/₄ cup	50 mL
Lettuce leaves	2-4	2-4

(continued on next page)

Heat tomatoes in saucepan. Mash until broken up. Add gelatin and Worcestershire sauce. Stir to dissolve gelatin. Cool.

Add apple and celery. Chill, stirring occasionally, until it begins to thicken. Pour into 2 cup (500 mL) mold. Chill until set.

Unmold onto lettuce leaves on plate. Makes 2 cups (450 mL).

Pictured on page 143.

NUTRITION GUIDE	¹/₃ cup/75 mL contains:	
	Energy	30 Calories (127 kJ)
	Cholesterol	0 mg
	Sodium	202 mg
	Fat	trace

VEGETABLE SALAD

Green and refreshing. A good mixture of vegetables.

SALAD

Torn or cut greens, packed (lettuce, romaine, spinach)	**4 cups**	**1 L**
Radishes, cut in tiny matchsticks	**4**	**4**
Medium carrot, finely grated	**1**	**1**
Alfalfa sprouts	**1 cup**	**225 mL**
Peas, fresh or frozen, thawed	**1 cup**	**225 mL**

VINEGAR DRESSING

Apple cider vinegar	**3 tbsp.**	**45 mL**
Liquid sweetener	**¹/₂ tsp.**	**2 mL**
Cooking oil	**1¹/₂ tsp.**	**7 mL**

Salad: Combine all vegetables in large bowl. Chill until ready to serve.

Vinegar Dressing: Mix vinegar, liquid sweetener and cooking oil. Pour over salad. Toss well. Makes about 7 cups (1.58 L) loosely packed salad.

NUTRITION GUIDE	1 cup/225 mL contains:	
	Energy	41 Calories (173 kJ)
	Cholesterol	0 mg
	Sodium	10 mg
	Fat	1 g

MACARONI SALAD

A salad with crunch and color.

Elbow macaroni	1½ cups	350 mL
Boiling water	2 qts.	2.5 L
Chopped celery	1 cup	225 mL
Chopped green pepper	½ cup	125 mL
Green onions, chopped	4	4
Chopped pimiento	2 tbsp.	30 mL
DRESSING		
Low-fat sour cream (7% MF)	¼ cup	50 mL
Light salad dressing (or mayonnaise)	¾ cup	175 mL

Cook macaroni in boiling water in large uncovered saucepan until tender but firm, about 5 to 7 minutes. Drain. Rinse with cold water. Drain well. Return to pot.

Add celery, green pepper, onion and pimiento. Stir to mix.

Dressing: Stir sour cream and salad dressing together in small bowl. Add to salad. Toss well. Makes 4½ cups (1.03 L).

NUTRITION GUIDE	½ cup/125 mL contains:	
	Energy	141 Calories (589 kJ)
	Cholesterol	3 mg
	Sodium	178 mg
	Fat	6 g

ORANGE SALAD

Very soft and fluffy. The orange flavored gelatin is added dry therefore gelatin does not set.

Envelope dessert topping	1	1
Skim milk	½ cup	115 mL
Low-fat cottage cheese (less than 1% MF), drained, smoothed in blender	1 cup	225 mL
Crushed pineapple, unsweetened, drained and pressed dry	14 oz.	398 mL
Low calorie orange flavored gelatin (jelly powder), 4 serving size	1	1

(continued on next page)

Beat topping and milk until stiff as directed on package.

Fold in cottage cheese and pineapple. Sprinkle dry gelatin over top. Fold in. Turn into ungreased 8 x 8 inch (20 x 20 cm) pan. Chill. Cuts into 9 servings.

NUTRITION GUIDE	1 serving contains:	
	Energy	70 Calories (293 kJ)
	Cholesterol	1 mg
	Sodium	128 mg
	Fat	2 g

MOLDED VEGETABLE SALAD

This contains pineapple as well as three vegetables.

Low calorie lime flavored gelatin (jelly powder), 4 serving size	1	1
Boiling water	³/₄ **cup**	175 mL
Crushed pineapple, unsweetened, with juice	14 oz.	398 mL
Onion flakes	2 tsp.	10 mL
Light salad dressing (or mayonnaise)	3 tbsp.	50 mL
Vinegar	2 tsp.	10 mL
Grated cabbage	¹/₂ **cup**	125 mL
Chopped celery	¹/₂ **cup**	125 mL
Grated carrot	¹/₄ **cup**	50 mL

Stir gelatin into boiling water until dissolved. Add pineapple with juice and onion flakes. Chill until syrupy. Stir occasionally.

Add salad dressing and vinegar. Whisk well to mix.

Add cabbage, celery and carrot. Pour into 4 cup (900 mL) salad mold. Chill. Makes 4 cups (900 mL).

NUTRITION GUIDE	¹/₃ cup/75 mL contains:	
	Energy	28 Calories (118 kJ)
	Cholesterol	0 mg
	Sodium	38 mg
	Fat	1 g

FRUIT SALAD PLATE

This makes a large pretty plateful. Serve with toast or dinner rolls for a full meal.

SWEET YOGURT DRESSING

Low-fat plain yogurt (less than 1% MF)	1 cup	225 mL
Brown sugar	4 tsp.	20 mL
Lemon juice	1 tsp.	5 mL
Vanilla	1/4 tsp.	1 mL
Liquid sweetener	1/4 tsp.	1 mL
Lettuce leaves, small	4	4
Low-fat cottage cheese (less than 1% MF)	2 cups	450 mL
Sliced strawberries	1 1/2 cups	350 mL
Bananas, sliced	2	2
Apple, sliced	1	1
Seedless grapes, halved	1 cup	225 mL
Melon, cut bite size (cantaloupe, honeydew, mango, watermelon)	3 cups	675 mL
Kiwifruit, cut bite size	1/2 cup	125 mL

Sweet Yogurt Dressing: Mix all 5 ingredients. Chill.

Put small leaf of lettuce in center of each plate. Put scoop of cottage cheese in center of lettuce .

Surround with next 6 fruits. Spoon dressing over fruit. Makes 4 servings.

N U T R I T I O N G U I D E	1 serving contains:	
	Energy	340 Calories (1424 kJ)
	Cholesterol	7 mg
	Sodium	561 mg
	Fat	3 g

Pare Pointer

If anyone has to be thrifty, let it be ancestors.

A colorful side salad that is perfect served with quiche. May be doubled for a main meal. Makes a good dessert.

Papaya (or cantaloupe), cut in balls (or bite size pieces)	**¹/₂ cup**	**125 mL**
Kiwifruit (or honeydew), cut in bite size pieces	**¹/₂ cup**	**125 mL**
Watermelon, cut in balls (or bite size pieces)	**¹/₂ cup**	**125 mL**
Strawberries, halved	**¹/₂ cup**	**125 mL**
Raspberries	**¹/₂ cup**	**125 mL**
Blueberries	**¹/₄ cup**	**60 mL**
ORANGE DRESSING		
Low-fat sour cream (7% MF)	**¹/₂ cup**	**60 mL**
Frozen concentrated orange juice, unsweetened	**1 tbsp.**	**15 mL**
Liquid sweetener	**¹/₂ tsp.**	**2 mL**
Chopped walnuts	**1 tbsp.**	**15 mL**

Combine all 6 fruits in bowl.

Orange Dressing: Mix all ingredients well. Pour over fruit. Toss lightly. Makes 2³/₄ cups (625 mL). Serves 4.

NUTRITION GUIDE	**1 serving contains:**	
	Energy	104 Calories (434 kJ)
	Cholesterol	12 mg
	Sodium	17 mg
	Fat	4 g

It is easy to recognize a fighting daisy. It will look like a blackeyed Susan.

CUCUMBER DRESSING

This also doubles as a dip for fresh vegetables.

Medium cucumber, peeled, seeded and grated	$1/2$	$1/2$
Low-fat plain yogurt (less than 1% MF)	**$1/2$ cup**	**125 mL**
Dill weed	**$1/8$ tsp.**	**0.5 mL**
Onion powder	**$1/8$ tsp.**	**0.5 mL**
Liquid sweetener	**$1/8$ tsp.**	**0.5 mL**
Salt	**$1/8$ tsp.**	**0.5 mL**

Place grated cucumber in sieve. Let drain 15 minutes. Press down once or twice. Turn into medium bowl.

Add yogurt, dill weed, onion powder, sweetener and salt. Stir. Makes $3/4$ cup (175 mL).

NUTRITION GUIDE	1 tbsp./15 mL contains:	
	Energy	8 Calories (31 kJ)
	Cholesterol	trace
	Sodium	37 mg
	Fat	trace

1. Scotch Scones page 31
2. Chicken In A Pot Soup page 128
3. Leek And Potato Soup page 133
4. Tomato Cabbage Soup page 132

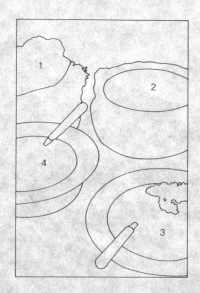

One of the easiest and best dressings for any greens. Extremely low in calories and fat. Simplify this salad another time, by using only lettuce, radish and onion.

SALAD

Crisp lettuce, cut or torn, lightly packed	6 cups	1.35 L
Grated carrot	¹/₂ cup	125 mL
Radishes, thinly sliced	6	6
Green onions, sliced	2	2
Medium tomato, diced	1	1
Slivered green pepper	¹/₄ cup	60 mL
Thinly sliced celery	¹/₃ cup	75 mL

OIL AND VINEGAR DRESSING

Vegetable cooking oil	1¹/₂ tsp.	7 mL
Vinegar	3 tbsp.	45 mL
Liquid sweetener	1 tbsp.	15 mL

Salad: Combine all ingredients in large bowl. Chill in refrigerator until shortly before serving.

Oil And Vinegar Dressing: Add cooking oil to salad just before serving. Toss to coat thoroughly.

Mix vinegar and sweetener together. Pour over lettuce. Toss. Serves 6.

NUTRITION GUIDE	**1 serving contains:**	
	Energy	33 Calories (137 kJ)
	Cholesterol	0 mg
	Sodium	20 mg
	Fat	1 g

Paré Pointer

Strange how hush money usually talks the loudest.

CHICKEN IN A POT SOUP

Serve with crusty buns for a complete meal. If on a sodium restricted diet, use low sodium canned soup in ingredients.

Chicken thighs, skin removed	1 lb.	454 g
Water	2$^1/_3$ cups	525 mL
Bay leaf	1	1
Salt	$^1/_2$ tsp.	2 mL
Pepper	$^1/_4$ tsp.	1 mL
Chopped onion	$^1/_2$ cup	125 mL
Fresh mushrooms, cut in 4 or 5 pieces	1 cup	250 mL
Condensed cream of chicken soup	10 oz.	284 mL
Grated carrot	1 cup	250 mL
Peas, fresh or frozen	1 cup	250 mL

Remove meat from bones and dice. Combine chicken, water, bay leaf, salt and pepper in medium saucepan. Bring to a boil. Simmer 30 minutes until meat is tender. Discard bay leaf.

Add onion, mushrooms, soup and carrot. Cover and simmer 20 to 30 minutes until vegetables are tender.

Add peas. Simmer 4 to 5 minutes. Makes about 6 cups (1.35 L).

Pictured on page 125.

NUTRITION GUIDE	1 cup contains:	
	Energy	229 Calories (958 kJ)
	Cholesterol	70 mg
	Sodium	708 mg
	Fat	10 g

Old mathematicians finally die when their numbers are up.

Lighter red than most. Lots of vegetables.

Canned beets, drained and diced (juice reserved)	**14 oz.**	**398 mL**
Beef bouillon packets (35% less salt)	**2 x ¹/₄ oz.**	**2 x 6.5 g**
Boiling water	**3¹/₂ cups**	**800 mL**
Coarsely grated cabbage, packed	**2 cups**	**450 mL**
Chopped onion	**1 cup**	**225 mL**
Thinly sliced carrots (use small size)	**1 cup**	**225 mL**
Ground cloves	**¹/₈ tsp.**	**0.5 mL**
Dill weed	**¹/₈ tsp.**	**0.5 mL**
Pepper	**¹/₈ tsp.**	**0.5 mL**
Reserved beets		
Low-fat plain yogurt (less than 1% MF)	**4 tbsp.**	**60 mL**

Drain beet juice into medium saucepan.

Bring beet juice to a boil. Add bouillon powder and boiling water. Stir to dissolve.

Add next 6 ingredients. Bring to a boil. Simmer covered about 25 minutes until cooked.

Add beets. Return to boiling just to heat beets.

Serve with a dollop of yogurt on top. Makes about 6¹/₈ cups (1.38 L).

NUTRITION GUIDE	1 cup/225 mL contains:	
	Energy	48 Calories (202 kJ)
	Cholesterol	trace
	Sodium	342 mg
	Fat	trace

VEGETABLE SOUP

A thick smooth soup. A dab of low-fat yogurt or sour cream may be stirred into each bowl.

Chopped potato	2 cups	450 mL
Chopped leeks, white part only	1¹/₂ cups	350 mL
Chopped carrot	¹/₂ cup	125 mL
Chopped zucchini, with peel	5 cups	1.13 L
Chopped celery	¹/₂ cup	125 mL
Peas, fresh or frozen	1 cup	225 mL
Water	4 cups	900 mL
Chicken bouillon packets (35% less salt)	4 × ¹/₄ oz.	4 × 6.5 g
Lemon juice	1 tsp.	5 mL
Tarragon	1 tsp.	5 mL
Parsley flakes	¹/₂ tsp.	2 mL
Pepper	¹/₈ tsp.	0.5 mL

Put potato, leeks, carrot, zucchini, celery, peas, water and chicken bouillon powder into large saucepan. Bring to a boil. Simmer gently, covered, for about 20 minutes until vegetables are cooked. Remove from heat. Cool for 15 minutes. Run through blender to smooth. You will need to blend in batches. Return to saucepan.

Add remaining ingredients. Return to a gentle simmer, about 5 minutes. Makes 5 cups (1.13 L).

NUTRITION GUIDE	**1 cup/225 mL contains:**	
	Energy	134 Calories (560 kJ)
	Cholesterol	trace
	Sodium	495 mg
	Fat	trace

TOMATO SOUP

This is an excellent first course. Good flavor. The easiest soup ever.

Tomato juice	2 cups	450 mL
Skim milk	3 cups	700 mL
Cornstarch	4 tbsp.	60 mL
Basil	³/₄ tsp.	4 mL

(continued on next page)

Stir all ingredients together in saucepan. Heat and stir until it boils and thickens. If too thick a bit of water may be added. Makes about 4 cups (900 mL).

NUTRITION GUIDE	1 cup/225 mL contains:	
	Energy	121 Calories (505 kJ)
	Cholesterol	4 mg
	Sodium	552 mg
	Fat	trace

CLAM CHOWDER

Good, full bodied chowder. Carrots add little bits of color.

Medium potatoes, diced	2	2
Grated carrot	1/2 cup	125 mL
Finely chopped onion	3/4 cup	175 mL
Celery flakes	1 tsp.	5 mL
Water	2 cups	450 mL
All-purpose flour	2 tbsp.	30 mL
Salt	1/2 tsp.	2 mL
Pepper	1/8 tsp.	0.5 mL
Skim milk	1 cup	225 mL
Canned chopped clams, with juice	5 oz.	142 g

Cook potato, carrot, onion and celery flakes in water about 10 minutes until vegetables are tender. Using potato masher, mash about 1/2 of vegetables in one side of pot.

Mix flour, salt and pepper in milk until smooth. Stir into boiling soup until it returns to a boil and thickens.

Add clams with juice. Heat through. Makes about 5 cups (1.13 L).

NUTRITION GUIDE	1 cup/225 mL contains:	
	Energy	110 Calories (462 kJ)
	Cholesterol	15 mg
	Sodium	351 mg
	Fat	trace

TOMATO CABBAGE SOUP

A full bodied soup. Deep in color.

Canned tomatoes	19 oz.	540 mL
Grated cabbage, packed	2 cups	450 mL
Chopped onion	1/2 cup	125 mL
Beef bouillon packets (35% less salt)	2 x 1/4 oz.	2 x 6.5 g
Boiling water	1 cup	250 mL
Liquid sweetener	1/4 tsp.	1 mL
Peas, fresh or frozen	1/4 cup	50 mL

Pour tomatoes into medium saucepan. Mash them well. Add cabbage and onion.

Dissolve bouillon powder in boiling water in cup. Add to saucepan. Bring to a boil. Cover. Simmer slowly for about 20 minutes until vegetables are tender.

Add sweetener and peas. Simmer 3 to 4 minutes to cook peas. Makes 4 cups (900 mL).

Pictured on page 125.

N U T R I T I O N G U I D E	1 cup/225 mL contains:	
	Energy	58 Calories (242 kJ)
	Cholesterol	trace
	Sodium	521 mg
	Fat	trace

QUICK SHRIMP SOUP

Quick and easy. Make from convenience foods. If on a sodium restricted diet, use low sodium canned soup in the ingredients.

Condensed cream of mushroom soup	10 oz.	284 mL
Skim milk	2 3/4 cups	625 mL
Canned broken shrimp, rinsed, drained and mashed	4 oz.	113 g
Cornstarch	2 tbsp.	30 mL
Hot pepper sauce	1/4 tsp.	1 mL

(continued on next page)

Whisk soup and milk together. Add remaining ingredients. Heat, stirring until it simmers. Makes 4 cups (900 mL).

NUTRITION GUIDE	1 cup/225 mL contains:	
	Energy	185 Calories (775 kJ)
	Cholesterol	5 mg
	Sodium	745 mg
	Fat	7 g

LEEK AND POTATO SOUP

This needn't be smooth but when run through the blender it takes on a better look. Good thick soup.

Chicken bouillon packets (35% less salt)	2 x ¼ oz.	2 x 6.5 g
Boiling water	2 cups	500 mL
Diced, peeled potatoes	1½ cups	350 mL
Chopped leeks, white part only	2½ cups	1.23 L
Chopped onion	2 tbsp.	30 mL
Skim milk	½ cup	125 mL
Chopped chives		
Freshly ground black pepper		

Dissolve bouillon powder in boiling water in medium saucepan.

Add potatoes, leeks and onion. Bring to a boil. Cover. Simmer slowly for about 30 minutes. If you want a smooth soup, run it through blender and return to saucepan.

Add skim milk. Heat through.

Garnish with chives and a generous sprinkle of freshly ground pepper. Makes 4 cups (900 mL).

Pictured on page 125.

NUTRITION GUIDE	1 cup/225 mL contains:	
	Energy	109 Calories (454 kJ)
	Cholesterol	1 mg
	Sodium	324 mg
	Fat	trace

CHEESY NOODLES

This has a light nip to offset the lack of salt. Sprinkle with salt if you like. More spice may also be added.

Fettuccini	**4 oz.**	**125 g**
Boiling water	**1½ qts.**	**2 L**
Low-fat cottage cheese (less than 1% MF)	**1 cup**	**225 mL**
Low-fat plain yogurt (less than 1% MF)	**½ cup**	**125 mL**
Finely chopped onion	**2 tbsp.**	**30 mL**
All-purpose flour	**1 tbsp.**	**15 mL**
Worcestershire sauce	**¼ tsp.**	**1 mL**
Onion powder	**⅛ tsp.**	**0.5 mL**
Garlic powder	**⅛ tsp.**	**0.5 mL**
Pepper	**⅛ tsp.**	**0.5 mL**

Paprika, good sprinkle

Cook fettuccini in boiling water in large uncovered saucepan about 5 to 7 minutes, until tender but firm. Drain. Return to pot.

Combine next 8 ingredients in bowl. Stir well. Add to noodles. Stir. Turn into 1 quart (1 L) casserole.

Sprinkle with paprika. Bake, uncovered, in 350°F (175°C) oven about 45 minutes. Makes generous 2½ cups (575 mL). Serves 2.

NUTRITION GUIDE	1 serving contains:	
	Energy	360 Calories (1506 kJ)
	Cholesterol	7 mg
	Sodium	600 mg
	Fat	2 g

Unfortunately, when a postman gets old he loses his zip.

A surprisingly good flavor with only noodles and yogurt as the main ingredients. Easy.

Fettuccini	**8 oz.**	**250 g**
Boiling water	**2¹/₂ qts.**	**3 L**
Low-fat plain yogurt (less than 1% MF)	**6 tbsp.**	**100 mL**
Salt	**¹/₄ tsp.**	**1 mL**
Pepper, sprinkle		
Parsley flakes	**¹/₂ tsp.**	**2 mL**
Grated Parmesan cheese	**2 tbsp.**	**30 mL**

Cook fettuccini in boiling water in large uncovered saucepan until tender but firm, about 9 to 11 minutes. Drain. Return to pot.

Add yogurt, salt, pepper and parsley flakes. Stir. Turn fettuccini into serving bowl.

Sprinkle with Parmesan cheese. Makes 3¹/₂ cups (800 mL).

NUTRITION GUIDE	1 cup/225 mL contains:	
	Energy	292 Calories (1221 kJ)
	Cholesterol	3 mg
	Sodium	272 mg
	Fat	2 g

The banker quit his job because he was bored. He lost interest in everything.

HARVARD BEETS

Get the sweet and sour taste without the sugar.

Fresh beets, cooked, peeled and diced (about 5 medium)	3 cups	700 mL
Water	2 cups	500 mL
Cornstarch	3 tbsp.	45 mL
Water	1 cup	225 mL
Vinegar	2 tbsp.	30 mL
Liquid sweetener	1½ tsp.	7 mL

Buy beets of the same size. Cook with skin intact in water until tender. Drain. Run cold water over beets until cool enough to handle. Slide skin off. Dice beets. You should have 3 cups (675 mL).

While beets are cooking combine cornstarch and water together in medium saucepan. Add vinegar and sweetener. Heat and stir until it boils and thickens. Add beets. Cover and remove from heat for about 15 minutes until sauce colors. Return to heat until heated through. Add a bit more water if too thick. Serves 6.

NUTRITION GUIDE	1 serving contains:	
	Energy	48 Calories (199 kJ)
	Cholesterol	0 mg
	Sodium	52 mg
	Fat	trace

MASHED PARSNIPS

Very tasty. The orange flavor comes through for a good variation.

Parsnips, peeled and cut bite size	1 lb.	454 g
Boiling water		
Prepared orange juice, unsweetened	⅓ cup	75 mL
Finely grated orange rind	¼ tsp.	1 mL
Cinnamon, just a pinch		
Nutmeg, just a pinch		
Liquid sweetener	½ tsp.	2 mL

(continued on next page)

Cook parsnips in boiling water until tender. Drain.

Add remaining ingredients. Mash well. Makes about 1½ cups (350 mL). Makes 4 servings.

1 serving contains:

Energy	95 Calories (397 kJ)
Cholesterol	0 mg
Sodium	12 mg
Fat	trace

ZUCCHINI

A good combination for both color and flavor.

Vegetable cooking oil	**1 tsp.**	**5 mL**
Chopped onion	**⅓ cup**	**75 mL**
Canned tomatoes	**1 cup**	**250 mL**
Zucchini with peel, cut in short strips	**3 cups**	**700 mL**
Granulated sugar	**½ tsp.**	**2 mL**

Heat cooking oil in saucepan. Add onion. Sauté until clear and soft.

Add tomatoes, zucchini and sugar. Cover and cook for about 10 minutes. Makes 1¾ cups (400 mL).

Pictured on page 143.

½ cup/125 mL contains:

Energy	51 Calories (215 kJ)
Cholesterol	0 mg
Sodium	122 mg
Fat	2 g

PEAS WITH MUSHROOMS

Good, with or without the addition of thyme. Try it both ways.

Finely chopped onion	$^1/_2$ cup	125 mL
Sliced, fresh mushrooms	2 cups	450 mL
Boiling water	1 cup	225 mL
Peas, fresh or frozen	3 cups	675 mL
Salt	$^1/_4$ tsp.	1 mL
Pepper, sprinkle		
Margarine	2 tsp.	10 mL
Thyme (optional)	$^1/_8$ tsp.	0.5 mL

Cook onion and mushrooms in boiling water for 10 minutes.

Add peas. Return to a boil. Cook for 4 minutes until tender. Drain.

Sprinkle with salt and pepper. Add margarine. Toss together. Add thyme if desired. Makes about 3 cups (675 mL).

Pictured on page 89.

NUTRITION GUIDE	$^1/_2$ cup/125 mL contains:	
	Energy	85 Calories (355 kJ)
	Cholesterol	0 mg
	Sodium	133 mg
	Fat	2 g

PARSNIP CAKES

Tasty little vegetable patties.

Large egg	1	1
Egg white (large)	1	1
All-purpose flour	$^1/_3$ cup	75 mL
Grated parsnips	1 cup	225 mL
Skim milk	$^1/_4$ cup	60 mL
Vegetable cooking oil	1 tsp.	5 mL

(continued on next page)

Beat egg, egg white and flour well with spoon in bowl.

Stir in parsnips and milk. Shape into 8 patties.

Heat cooking oil in frying pan. Brown cakes on both sides. Do not have pan too hot so parsnips will cook as cakes brown. Makes 8. Serves 4, allowing 2 cakes each.

NUTRITION GUIDE	1 serving (2 cakes) contains:	
	Energy	105 Calories (439 kJ)
	Cholesterol	54 mg
	Sodium	42 mg
	Fat	3 g

CARROT MAGIC

Like a sweet and sour orange sauce.

Carrots, peeled, cut up	**1 lb.**	**454 g**
Boiling water		
Frozen concentrated orange juice, unsweetened	**¹/₄ cup**	**60 mL**
Water	**¹/₄ cup**	**60 mL**
Cornstarch	**1 tsp.**	**5 mL**
Liquid sweetener	**1 tsp.**	**5 mL**

Cook carrots in boiling water until tender. Drain.

Combine concentrated orange juice, water, cornstarch and sweetener in small bowl. Pour over carrots. Heat and stir until it boils and thickens. Makes 2¹/₂ cups (575 mL).

Pictured on page 89.

NUTRITION GUIDE	¹/₂ cup/125 mL contains:	
	Energy	65 Calories (273 kJ)
	Cholesterol	0 mg
	Sodium	32 mg
	Fat	trace

MASHED CARROT DISH: Mash cooked carrots. Add 1 tbsp. (15 mL) frozen concentrated orange juice. Mash and taste adding more orange juice if desired. A nice change in texture.

CORN CASSEROLE

Thick and custardy, even without eggs.

Margarine	1 tbsp.	15 mL
Chopped onion	¼ cup	60 mL
All-purpose flour	2 tbsp.	30 mL
Skim milk	½ cup	125 mL
Pepper	⅛ tsp.	0.5 mL
Cream style corn	14 oz.	398 mL
TOPPING		
Margarine	1 tbsp.	15 mL
Dry bread crumbs	¼ cup	60 mL

Melt margarine in frying pan. Add onion. Sauté until soft and clear.

Sprinkle with flour. Mix. Stir in skim milk and pepper until it boils and thickens.

Add corn. Stir. Pour into 1 quart (1L) casserole.

Topping: Melt margarine in small saucepan. Stir in bread crumbs. Sprinkle over casserole. Bake, uncovered, in 350°F (175°C) oven about 30 minutes until browned. Makes 2 cups (450 mL).

NUTRITION GUIDE	½ cup/125 mL contains:	
	Energy	186 Calories (778 kJ)
	Cholesterol	1 mg
	Sodium	443 mg
	Fat	7 g

MACARONI AND TOMATOES

A good tasty old stand-by.

Macaroni	2 cups	450 mL
Boiling water	3 qts.	4 L
Skim milk	¼ cup	60 mL
Margarine	1 tbsp.	15 mL
Pepper	⅛ tsp.	0.5 mL
Canned tomatoes	14 oz.	398 mL

(continued on next page)

Cook macaroni in boiling water in large uncovered Dutch oven about 5 to 6 minutes, until tender but firm. Drain. Return macaroni to pot.

Add milk, margarine and pepper. Toss.

Heat tomatoes in separate saucepan. Pour over macaroni. Stir. Makes 5 cups (1.13 L).

NUTRITION GUIDE	**1 cup/225 mL contains:**	
	Energy	206 Calories (860 kJ)
	Cholesterol	trace
	Sodium	168 mg
	Fat	3 g

BAKED TOMATOES

Adding onion, chopped egg white and a bit of beef, helps to make this very tasty.

Canned tomatoes	**14 oz.**	**398 mL**
Chopped onion	**¹/₃ cup**	**75 mL**
Dry bread crumbs	**1 cup**	**225 mL**
Cooked roast beef, cubed, all visible fat removed	**¹/₂ cup**	**125 mL**
Large hard-boiled eggs, whites only, chopped	**2**	**2**
Granulated sugar	**¹/₂ tsp.**	**2 mL**
Pepper	**¹/₈ tsp.**	**0.5 mL**

Combine tomatoes and onion in saucepan. Bring to a boil. Simmer for about 15 minutes until onion is tender. Remove from heat.

Stir in bread crumbs and beef.

Add egg whites, sugar and pepper. Stir. Pour into 1 quart (1 L) casserole. Bake, uncovered, in 350°F (175°C) oven for about 35 to 40 minutes. Makes 2 cups (450 mL).

NUTRITION GUIDE	**¹/₂ cup/125 mL contains:**	
	Energy	179 Calories (750 kJ)
	Cholesterol	12 mg
	Sodium	415 mg
	Fat	3 g

SAUTÉED CABBAGE

An economical vegetable. It has a very faint hint of sauerkraut flavor.

Chopped or sliced onion	³/₄ **cup**	**175 mL**
Water	³/₄ **cup**	**175 mL**
Grated cabbage, packed	**4 cups**	**900 mL**
Vegetable cooking oil	**1 tbsp.**	**15 mL**
Vinegar	**1 tbsp.**	**15 mL**

Combine onion and water in frying pan. Cover. Simmer until soft.

Add cabbage. Stir. Add more water if needed. Simmer about 6 minutes until cabbage is tender crisp.

Add cooking oil and vinegar. Stir-fry about 20 to 25 minutes until coated and water has boiled away. Makes 2 cups (450 mL).

NUTRITION GUIDE	¹/₂ **cup/125 mL contains:**	
	Energy	61 Calories (254 kJ)
	Cholesterol	0 mg
	Sodium	14 mg
	Fat	4 g

SCALLOPED CELERY WITH TOMATO

If you are used to having your celery cold, you will want to try this.

Sliced celery	5 cups	1.1 L
Canned tomatoes, reserve ¼ cup (50 mL) juice	14 oz.	398 mL
Finely chopped onion	1 cup	250 mL
Granulated sugar	2 tsp.	10 mL
Salt	¼ tsp.	1 mL
Pepper	¼ tsp.	1 mL
All-purpose flour	2 tbsp.	30 mL
Reserved tomato juice	¼ cup	50 mL
Margarine	2 tbsp.	30 mL
Cracker crumbs	½ cup	125 mL

Combine first 6 ingredients in medium saucepan. Simmer, covered, for 5 minutes.

In small cup, mix flour and reserved tomato juice until no lumps remain. Stir into tomato mixture until it returns to a boil. Pour into 2 quart (2.5 L) casserole.

Melt margarine in small saucepan. Stir in cracker crumbs. Sprinkle over casserole. Bake, uncovered, in 350°F (175°C) oven about 25 to 30 minutes until hot and browned. Makes 4½ cups (1 L).

NUTRITION GUIDE	½ cup/125 mL contains:	
	Energy	84 Calories (351 kJ)
	Cholesterol	trace
	Sodium	285 mg
	Fat	3 g

Paré Pointer

Posted over a swimming pool, "If you drink, don't dive."

FETTUCCINI

Quick to prepare. Red pepper and peas add color.

Fettuccini	1 lb.	454 g
Boiling water	4 qts.	5 L
Margarine	2 tbsp.	30 mL
Frozen peas, thawed	1½ cups	350 mL
Red pepper, slivered	1	1
All-purpose flour	2 tbsp.	30 mL
Skim milk	1 cup	225 mL
Grated Parmesan cheese	6 tbsp.	90 mL

Cook fettuccini in boiling water in large uncovered pot until tender but firm about 9 to 11 minutes. Drain. Return fettuccini to pot.

Meanwhile heat margarine in frying pan. Add peas and red pepper. Sauté about 4 minutes until tender.

Sprinkle with flour. Mix. Stir in skim milk until it boils. Pour over drained fettuccini. Divide among 6 plates.

Sprinkle each plate with Parmesan cheese. Makes 9 cups (2.03 L). Serves 6.

Pictured on page 143.

NUTRITION GUIDE	1 serving contains:	
	Energy	386 Calories (1617 kJ)
	Cholesterol	5 mg
	Sodium	206 mg
	Fat	7 g

OVEN BAKED FRIES

Crispy good.

Medium baking potatoes, peeled and cut in strips	3	3
Vegetable cooking oil	1 tbsp.	15 mL

(continued on next page)

Coat baking sheet with no-stick cooking spray. Put potato strips into large bowl. Drizzle with cooking oil. Toss together well to coat. Arrange on baking sheet. Bake in single layer in 450°F (230°C) oven for 15 minutes. Turn and bake about 10 to 15 minutes longer. Test a strip for crispness. Makes 4 servings.

Pictured on page 107.

NUTRITION GUIDE	1 serving contains:	
	Energy	35 Calories (146 kJ)
	Cholesterol	0 mg
	Sodium	2 mg
	Fat	trace

CARROT BAKE

Grated carrot and bread crumbs give this a different texture.

All-purpose flour	2 tbsp.	30 mL
Skim milk	1½ cups	375 mL
Chicken bouillon packet (35% less salt)	1 × ¼ oz.	1 × 6.5 g
Grated carrot	2 cups	500 mL
Dry bread crumbs	1 cup	250 mL
Finely chopped onion	⅓ cup	75 mL
Egg whites (large)	2	2
Pepper	¼ tsp.	1 mL

Spoon flour into medium saucepan. Stir in small amount of milk until smooth then add rest of milk. Add bouillon powder. Heat and stir until it boils and thickens. Remove from heat.

Stir in carrot and bread crumbs. Add remaining ingredients. Mix. Turn into 1 quart casserole. Bake, uncovered, in 350°F (175°C) oven for about 45 minutes until set and browned. Makes 2⅔ cups (600 mL).

NUTRITION GUIDE	½ cup/125 mL contains:	
	Energy	153 Calories (639 kJ)
	Cholesterol	2 mg
	Sodium	341 mg
	Fat	1 g

CELERY BAKE

Low calorie celery with onion added for flavor. Contains chopped egg whites. Very good.

Sliced celery	**1¹/₂ cups**	**350 mL**
Sliced onion	**1 cup**	**225 mL**
Boiling water		
Large hard boiled eggs, whites only, coarsely chopped	**3**	**3**
All-purpose flour	**2¹/₂ tbsp.**	**40 mL**
Skim milk	**1¹/₄ cups**	**275 mL**
Pepper	**¹/₈ tsp.**	**0.5 mL**
Paprika	**¹/₈ tsp.**	**0.5 mL**
Cayenne pepper, sprinkle		
Margarine	**2 tbsp.**	**30 mL**
Dry bread crumbs	**¹/₂ cup**	**125 mL**

Cook celery and onion in boiling water until tender. Drain. Turn into 1 quart (1 L) casserole.

Scatter egg white over top.

Measure flour into saucepan. Whisk in part of the milk until smooth. Add remaining milk, pepper, paprika and cayenne pepper. Heat and stir until it boils and thickens. Pour over casserole. Lift vegetables here and there so a bit of sauce goes to the bottom.

Melt margarine in small saucepan. Stir in bread crumbs. Spread over top. Bake, uncovered, in 350°F (175°C) oven for about 20 to 30 minutes until browned and hot. Makes about 2³/₄ cups (625 mL). Serves 5.

NUTRITION GUIDE	**1 serving contains:**	
	Energy	152 Calories (634 kJ)
	Cholesterol	1 mg
	Sodium	237 mg
	Fat	5 g

A good size casserole. An easy way to get cabbage roll flavor with little preparation.

Long grain rice	1½ cups	050 mL
Water	3 cups	675 mL
Vegetable cooking oil	1 tbsp.	15 mL
Chopped onion	½ cup	125 mL
Coarsely grated cabbage, packed	2 cups	450 mL
All-purpose flour	1 tbsp.	15 mL
Canned tomatoes	1 cup	250 mL
Low-fat plain yogurt (less than 1% MF)	½ cup	125 mL
Granulated sugar	½ tsp.	2 mL
Salt	½ tsp.	2 mL
Pepper	¼ tsp.	1 mL
Boiling water	½ cup	125 mL

Cook rice in first amount of water about 15 minutes, until tender.

Heat cooking oil in large frying pan. Add onion and cabbage. Stir fry until onion is soft.

Sprinkle with flour. Stir.

Add remaining ingredients and rice. Mix. Pour into 3 quart (4 L) casserole. Bake, covered, for 1 hour in 350°F (175°C) oven. Makes about 7⅓ cups (1.65 L).

NUTRITION GUIDE	½ cup/125 mL contains:	
	Energy	97 Calories (404 kJ)
	Cholesterol	trace
	Sodium	130
	Fat	1 g

Paré Pointer

King Arthur found his entertainment in a knight club.

ZUCCHINI CASSEROLE

Contains vegetables and cottage cheese. Cottage cheese is blender-smooth. You don't know it's in there.

Skim milk	1 cup	250 mL
All-purpose flour	1/4 cup	60 mL
Salt	1/2 tsp.	2 mL
Fresh, sliced mushrooms	2 cups	450 mL
Low-fat cottage cheese (less than 1% MF), smoothed in blender	1 cup	250 mL
Zucchini, cut bite size	5 cups	1.13 L
Grated carrot, packed	1 cup	250 mL
Sliced green onion	1/3 cup	75 mL
Thyme	1/4 tsp.	1 mL
TOPPING		
Margarine	2 tbsp.	30 mL
Dry bread crumbs	1/2 cup	125 mL
Grated low-fat sharp Cheddar cheese (less than 21% MF)	1/2 cup	125 mL

Stir milk, flour and salt until smooth in medium saucepan. Stir over medium heat until it boils and thickens.

Stir in sliced mushrooms and cottage cheese. Add zucchini, carrot, onion and thyme. Turn into 3 quart (4 L) casserole.

Topping: Melt margarine in small saucepan. Stir in bread crumbs and cheese. Sprinkle over top. Bake, uncovered, in 350°F (175°C) oven about 45 minutes, until cooked and browned. Makes about 5 1/2 cups (1.24 L).

NUTRITION GUIDE	1/2 cup/125 mL contains:	
	Energy	108 Calories (450 kJ)
	Cholesterol	5 mg
	Sodium	384 mg
	Fat	4 g

METRIC CONVERSION

Throughout this book measurements are given in Conventional and Metric measure. To compensate for differences between the two measurements due to rounding, a full metric measure is not always used. The cup used is the standard 8 fluid ounce. Temperature is given in degrees Fahrenheit and Celsius. Baking pan measurements are in inches and centimetres as well as quarts and litres. An exact metric conversion is given below as well as the working equivalent (Standard Measure).

OVEN TEMPERATURES

Fahrenheit (°F)	Celsius (°C)
175°	80°
200°	95°
225°	110°
250°	120°
275°	140°
300°	150°
325°	160°
350°	175°
375°	190°
400°	205°
425°	220°
450°	230°
475°	240°
500°	260°

SPOONS

Conventional Measure	Metric Exact Conversion Millilitre (mL)	Metric Standard Measure Millilitre (mL)
1/4 teaspoon (tsp.)	1.2 mL	1 mL
1/2 teaspoon (tsp.)	2.4 mL	2 mL
1 teaspoon (tsp.)	4.7 mL	5 mL
2 teaspoons (tsp.)	9.4 mL	10 mL
1 tablespoon (tbsp.)	14.2 mL	15 mL

CUPS

1/4 cup (4 tbsp.)	56.8 mL	50 mL
1/3 cup (51/3 tbsp.)	75.6 mL	75 mL
1/2 cup (8 tbsp.)	113.7 mL	125 mL
2/3 cup (102/3 tbsp.)	151.2 mL	150 mL
3/4 cup (12 tbsp.)	170.5 mL	175 mL
1 cup (16 tbsp.)	227.3 mL	250 mL
41/2 cups	1022.9 mL	1000 mL (1 L)

DRY MEASUREMENTS

Ounces (oz.)	Grams (g)	Grams (g)
1 oz.	28.3 g	30 g
2 oz.	56.7 g	55 g
3 oz.	85.0 g	85 g
4 oz.	113.4 g	125 g
5 oz.	141.7 g	140 g
6 oz.	170.1 g	170 g
7 oz.	198.4 g	200 g
8 oz.	226.8 g	250 g
16 oz.	453.6 g	500 g
32 oz.	907.2 g	1000 g (1 kg)

PANS, CASSEROLES

Conventional Inches	Metric Centimetres	Conventional Quart (qt.)	Metric Litre (L)
8x8 inch	20x20 cm	12/3 qt.	2 L
9x9 inch	22x22 cm	2 qt.	2.5 L
9x13 inch	22x33 cm	31/3 qt.	4 L
10x15 inch	25x38 cm	1 qt.	1.2 L
11x17 inch	28x43 cm	11/4 qt.	1.5 L
8x2 inch round	20x5 cm	12/3 qt.	2 L
9x2 inch round	22x5 cm	2 qt.	2.5 L
10x41/2 inch tube	25x11 cm	41/4 qt.	5 L
8x4x3 inch loaf	20x10x7 cm	11/4 qt.	1.5 L
9x5x3 inch loaf	23x12x7 cm	12/3 qt.	2 L

INDEX

If you don't see Company's Coming where you shop, ask your retailer to give us a call. Meanwhile, we offer a mail order service for your convenience.

Just indicate the books you would like below. Then complete the reverse page and send your order with payment to us.

Buying a gift? Enclose a personal note or card and we will be pleased to send it with your order.

Deduct $5.00 for every $35.00 ordered.
See reverse.

SAVE $5.00!

COOKBOOKS

Company's Coming Publishing Limited
Box 8037, Station F
Edmonton, Alberta, Canada T6H 4N9
Tel: (403) 450-6223

MAIL ORDER COUPON

QUANTITY • HARD COVER BOOK •

		TOTAL BOOKS	TOTAL PRICE
	Jean Paré's Favorites - Volume One		$

TOTAL $17.95 + $1.50 shipping = **$19.45 each** x ___ = $ ___

QUANTITY • SOFT COVER BOOKS •

150 Delicious Squares	Pasta
Casseroles	Cakes
Muffins & More	Barbecues
Salads	Dinners of the World
Appetizers	Lunches
Desserts	Pies
Soups & Sandwiches	Light Recipes
Holiday Entertaining	Microwave Cooking
Cookies	Preserves
Vegetables	Light Casseroles *(Sept.'94)*
Main Courses	

TOTAL BOOKS / TOTAL PRICE

TOTAL $10.95 + $1.50 shipping = **$12.45 each** x ___ = $ ___

QUANTITY • PINT SIZE BOOKS •

Finger Food
Party Planning
Buffets

TOTAL BOOKS / TOTAL PRICE

TOTAL $4.99 + $1.00 shipping = **$5.99 each** x ___ = $ ___

QUANTITY • SOFT COVER BOOKS •

150 délicieux carrés	Recettes légères
Les casseroles	Les salades
Muffins et plus	La cuisson au micro-ondes
Les dîners	Les pâtes
Les barbecues	Les conserves
Les tartes	Les casseroles légères *(sept.'94)*
Délices des fêtes	

TOTAL BOOKS / TOTAL PRICE

TOTAL $10.95 + $1.50 shipping = **$12.45 each** x ___ = $ ___

Please fill in reverse side of this coupon

TOTAL PRICE FOR ALL BOOKS *(See reverse)* * $ ___

Deduct $5.00 for every $35.00 ordered.

COOKBOOKS

Company's Coming Publishing Limited
Box 8037, Station F
Edmonton, Alberta, Canada T6H 4N9
Tel: (403) 450-6223

MAIL ORDER COUPON

TOTAL PRICE FOR ALL BOOKS (from reverse)	$
Less $5.00 for every $35.00 ordered	− $
SUBTOTAL	$
Canadian residents add G.S.T.	+ $
TOTAL AMOUNT ENCLOSED	$

- **MAKE CHEQUE OR MONEY ORDER PAYABLE TO:** *COMPANY'S COMING PUBLISHING LIMITED*

- **ORDERS OUTSIDE CANADA:** *Must be paid in U.S. funds by cheque or money order drawn on Canadian or U.S. bank.*

- *Prices subject to change without prior notice.*

- *Sorry, no C.O.D.'s*

Gift Giving

- Let us help you with your gift giving!
- We will send cookbooks directly to the recipients of your choice if you give us their names and addresses.
- Be sure to specify the titles of the cookbooks you wish to send to each person.
- If you would like to enclose your personal note or card, we will be pleased to include it with your gift order.

GIFT SHIPPING ADDRESS

Send my gift of Company's Coming Cookbooks listed on the reverse side of this coupon, to:

Name:

Street:

City: Province/State:

Postal Code/Zip: Tel: ( ) —

Company's Coming Cookbooks make excellent gifts. Birthdays, bridal showers, Mother's Day Father's Day, graduation or any occasion... collect them all! Remember to enclose your personal note or card and we will be pleased to send it with your order.

If you don't see Company's Coming where you shop, ask your retailer to give us a call. Meanwhile, we offer a mail order service for your convenience.

Just indicate the books you would like below. Then complete the reverse page and send your order with payment to us.

Buying a gift? Enclose a personal note or card and we will be pleased to send it with your order.

Deduct $5.00 for every $35.00 ordered.

See reverse.

SAVE $5.00!

COOKBOOKS

Company's Coming Publishing Limited
Box 8037, Station F
Edmonton, Alberta, Canada T6H 4N9
Tel: (403) 450-6223

MAIL ORDER COUPON

QUANTITY • HARD COVER BOOK •

Jean Paré's Favorites -
Volume One

TOTAL BOOKS   **TOTAL PRICE**

TOTAL $17.95 + $1.50 shipping = **$19.45 each** x ____ = $ ____

QUANTITY • SOFT COVER BOOKS •

150 Delicious Squares	Pasta
Casseroles	Cakes
Muffins & More	Barbecues
Salads	Dinners of the World
Appetizers	Lunches
Desserts	Pies
Soups & Sandwiches	Light Recipes
Holiday Entertaining	Microwave Cooking
Cookies	Preserves
Vegetables	Light Casseroles *(Sept.'94)*
Main Courses	

TOTAL BOOKS   **TOTAL PRICE**

TOTAL $10.95 + $1.50 shipping = **$12.45 each** x ____ = $ ____

QUANTITY • PINT SIZE BOOKS •

Finger Food
Party Planning
Buffets

TOTAL BOOKS   **TOTAL PRICE**

TOTAL $4.99 + $1.00 shipping = **$5.99 each** x ____ = $ ____

QUANTITY • SOFT COVER BOOKS •

150 délicieux carrés	Recettes légères
Les casseroles	Les salades
Muffins et plus	La cuisson au micro-ondes
Les dîners	Les pâtes
Les barbecues	Les conserves
Les tartes	Les casseroles légères *(sept.'94)*
Délices des fêtes	

TOTAL BOOKS   **TOTAL PRICE**

TOTAL $10.95 + $1.50 shipping = **$12.45 each** x ____ = $ ____

Please fill in reverse side of this coupon   **TOTAL PRICE FOR ALL BOOKS** *(See reverse)* * $ ____

SAVE $5.00!

Deduct $5.00 for every $35.00 ordered.

COOKBOOKS

Company's Coming Publishing Limited
Box 8037, Station F
Edmonton, Alberta, Canada T6H 4N9
Tel: (403) 450-6223

MAIL ORDER COUPON

TOTAL PRICE FOR ALL BOOKS (from reverse)	$
Less $5.00 for every $35.00 ordered −	$
SUBTOTAL	$
Canadian residents add G.S.T. +	$
TOTAL AMOUNT ENCLOSED	$

- **MAKE CHEQUE OR MONEY ORDER PAYABLE TO:** *COMPANY'S COMING PUBLISHING LIMITED*

- **ORDERS OUTSIDE CANADA:** *Must be paid in U.S. funds by cheque or money order drawn on Canadian or U.S. bank.*

- *Prices subject to change without prior notice.*

- *Sorry, no C.O.D.'s*

Gift Giving

- Let us help you with your gift giving!
- We will send cookbooks directly to the recipients of your choice if you give us their names and addresses.
- Be sure to specify the titles of the cookbooks you wish to send to each person.
- If you would like to enclose your personal note or card, we will be pleased to include it with your gift order.

GIFT SHIPPING ADDRESS

Send my gift of Company's Coming Cookbooks listed on the reverse side of this coupon, to:

Name:

Street:

City: Province/State:

Postal Code/Zip: Tel: (   )   —

Company's Coming Cookbooks make excellent gifts. Birthdays, bridal showers, Mother's Day, Father's Day, graduation or any occasion... collect them all! Remember to enclose your personal note or card and we will be pleased to send it with your order.